W9-BCF-889

ABRAHAM, LOVED BY GOD

This is VOLUME ONE of
THE BIBLE IN HISTORY
A Contemporary Companion to the Bible

Edited by Father Robert Tamisier, P.S.S.
Advisory Editor for the English Language Edition: Joseph Rhymer
Editorial Consultants:
Father Edward J. Ciuba
Bishop John J. Dougherty
Rabbi Samuel Sandmel
Dr Samuel L. Terrien

CONTENTS

PREFACE

The Bible is a single book in which the pattern of God's work in his world can be traced through two thousand years of human history. There is a single pattern running through it all, and fundamentally it is a simple pattern. The complexity comes from the complexity of human history.

But the Bible is also a collection of books. Some of them grew out of folk tales, and stories from the nation's past, which were handed down from father to son, or told round the pilgrims' camp fires at the places where the people went to worship. Some of the books were written by men who can be named and placed in their historical situation, and some are anonymous and can only be given a firm date with difficulty. The whole collection grew slowly over many centuries, and was repeatedly edited and rearranged, until it reached the form in which we now have it.

This means that the Bible has never been a book which could be read without help. Even in New Testament times, people found parts of it obscure. Customs which are taken for granted, and ways of life which are accepted without question by people who have never known anything different, may be strange to the later reader and difficult to understand. This is more than ever true in our own times, when the society in which we live has changed so much, even during the last hundred years.

This present series of books is for use as a Companion to the Bible. They are not a substitute for the Bible, for nothing can take the place of the Bible itself. It impresses itself on those who read it seriously in a way that no other book can. Some of the difficulties about reading the Bible have been due to the way in which it has usually been printed. Many of these are overcome in the Jerusalem Bible, a translation in contemporary English which is used in this series. In the Jerusalem Bible the text is presented by dividing the books into sections, and providing headings and footnotes.

The aim of this present series of books is to help people to understand the divine revelation. It presents the Bible in the historical circumstances in which it developed. The men and women who were so acutely aware of God's active presence in their lives were all people of their times. Their experiences were the same as the experiences of their neighbours and fellow-countrymen. They earned their living by the same skills and trades, and their thoughts were expressed in the language used by everyone around them. To understand how God was revealing himself to these people, we must share their experiences as far as we can, and know what was happening in the world in which they lived.

Using the findings of archaeology and of historical research, the books in this series show the circumstances and the environment in which God made himself known. During recent years great advances have been made in our knowledge of the Near East during the period when the Bible was written, but these advances have only been possible because of the foundations laid patiently by scholars for more than a hundred years.

This series of books does not attempt to record all of the most recent finds, for new discoveries often have to be examined with caution before there can be certainty about their significance. Only those views which are accepted by a wide range of scholars are used here. It is impressive and reassuring to see how far the discoveries of the archaeologists and historians have confirmed the authenticity of details given in the Bible. Again and again, objects have been discovered, and sites have been excavated, which have confirmed the picture given by the Bible itself. There are many hindrances to archaeological work in the Near East. Political frontiers are often real barriers, and many important sites are still centres of worship where a thorough investigation is not possible. But we can be confident that new discoveries, as they are confirmed and analysed, will deepen our understanding of the times when the foundations of our religion were laid.

It is sometimes thought that books such as these should attempt to give the historical background to the Bible without any mention of God. This is impossible. The Bible is history, but it is also sacred history. It is history viewed and written with the knowledge that God is the active source of all history, and that all events are part of the movement towards the final consummation which God has willed. There is a pattern in the events of history, and God shows himself through this pattern. The events will not make sense, nor will they be worth studying, unless we see them from the point of view of the people who found God in them. We cannot make sense of the events if we leave God out.

The modern reader is sometimes surprised by the strange ways in which ancient historians presented their material, but much of this strangeness comes from the way in which ancient authors set about their task. Many of the writers of the Bible felt that their main responsibility was to preserve the traditions and the accounts of the events with as little alteration as possible. They were 'scribes' rather than authors. They copied out whatever information they could find, or selected the best descriptions and the parts that they thought mattered most. Then they stitched the pieces together without changing the words or the style.

They collected their information wherever they could find it, so their work contains poetry, epics, fiction, official chronicles, anecdotes, family and tribal memoirs, royal decrees, codes of law, letters, rules for priests. These, and many others, are the kind of sources which historians use in any age; they are the raw material of history, and without them the historian would be helpless. But in the ancient historian's writings this raw material has a marked effect on the way in which the history is written. There is much repetition and, sometimes, contradiction, when the 'author' uses two versions of the same event. But there is also a vivid immediacy about it all which helps us to come close to the people who took part in the event and to appreciate the effect it had upon them.

The account is presented to us in the people's own words, so we find that we can share more easily in their experiences, and appreciate more easily their point of view. It is the point of view of a people who recognised God's active presence, and who responded to his presence with worship.

Occasionally we can detect a further motive which has shaped some of the books of the Bible. The biblical writers were never mere historians. They only wrote about the past if it could throw light on their present situation. They wanted to show how God had acted in the past, so that the people of their own times could see God's presence and power at work in their own lives. So the biblical historians selected from the material available, and then arranged it so that the lessons were as obvious as it was possible to make them.

When we read these passages we are seeing the events of history through the eyes of men who frequently were writing about those events many generations after they had occurred. The books they wrote were expressions of the faith of the men who wrote them, and they were written to strengthen the faith of the people who read them. They have more to say about that faith than they have about the historical details of the events on which that faith was built.

Sometimes the books of the Bible contain deliberate anachronisms. This can be seen, for example, in some of the words and actions attributed to Moses. Moses had a greater influence on the Hebrew people than any other man. Later, in times of urgent need or of national reform, it was only natural for men to ask themselves what Moses would have done if he had been faced with their problems. The action taken, or the programme of reform, was then recorded as if Moses himself had foreseen the situation and had legislated for it. This is why so much of the law is written as if it had been given by Moses.

The men who wrote in this way were expressing an important truth. Whenever the nation was unfaithful to God, it was because it had forgotten the principles which Moses had taught to his generation of Hebrews. Those principles lay at the heart of the Hebrew faith, but the people of each new generation had to apply them to the changing circumstances of their times. The convention of making Moses the author of all their laws was the clearest way of showing that those laws were expressions of the central traditions of the nation.

The people of the Bible recognised the thread of God's revelation in the ordinary events of their lives. This series of books shows what those events were, and how that thread fits into its historical background. Each book may be read on its own, but the books are also linked together to form a continuous exposition and elucidation of the way in which God has made himself known through the Bible. The titles in the series are:

Each book contains the necessary maps, diagrams and illustrations for the period with which it is concerned. The reader is also recommended to use the chronological table, the maps and the general information printed after the New Testament in the Jerusalem Bible Standard Edition.

Joseph Rhymer,
Editor of the English Language Edition.

1

UR: THE STARTING-POINT

Terah took his son Abram,[1] his grandson Lot the son of Haran, and his daughter in law Sarai the wife of Abram, and made them leave Ur of the Chaldaeans to go to the land of Canaan.[2] (Gen. 11:31)

This biblical annotation, with which the story of Abram begins, stands out with all the clarity of an etching, possibly with too much clarity for our taste. And so, as a historian, and with the help of the archaeological information which we possess at the present time, I shall try to reconstruct this scene, at least in its principal features.

Approximate date of the event: 1850 B.C.

Setting: the plain, near the city of Ur, in the delta of the Euphrates (map, pp. 2 and 3), skirting the Persian Gulf.

Ur was a city-state, the local capital, which was surrounded — like all the important urban centres of central and southern Mesopotamia of that period — by luxuriant vegetation encroaching on the desert. This agricultural wealth was obtained by a complicated and highly organized system of irrigation channels fed from the waters of the Euphrates. Right at the edge of this

[1] We shall see later (p. 117) in what circumstances his primitive name of Abram was changed to Abraham and, on the same occasion, the name of Sarai into Sarah.

[2] The land of Canaan (or Chanaan) is the name given by the Bible to the natural region occupied by Palestine.

THE FERTILE CRESCENT AND THE GENERAL OUTLINE OF ABRAM'S MIGRATION

This map is intended to show the general setting of Abram's great migration in about the year 1850 B.C.

Ur, the starting-place, in the delta of the Euphrates.

Purpose of this journey: to go to the Land of Canaan (nowadays Palestine, or the Holy Land).

It will be noticed that the journey of the small Hebrew party took place entirely within the region called the 'Fertile Crescent' (shown here as grey).

The journey took place in three phases:

(a) Up the right bank of the Euphrates (to avoid crossing the Syro-Arabian desert which would have proved deadly for the flocks).

(b) A fairly long halt in the Haran region (Paddan-aram).

(c) Down towards the southern part of the land of Canaan (through Shechem, Bethel, Hebron).

The map also shows the short journey into Egypt by Abram and his flocks.

agricultural nucleus, in which cereal cultivation pre-
dominated, ran a narrow belt of rather poor pasture; this
was a semi-desert area which the local farmers left to the
wandering shepherds who were always ready to fold or
put up their tents. These shepherds were unattractive
characters in the eyes of local farmers because, it seems,
they had a reputation for petty theft.

And so, on the plain bordering the cultivated fields,
Terah's shepherds and those of Abram, his son, began to
pull out the pegs and take down the tents. They were
black tents, woven from goat's hair. The donkeys —
stocky beasts with wiry legs — carried the baggage:
carpets, weapons (staves, javelins, bows and arrows),
kitchen utensils of a rudimentary kind, water-skins filled
with water and milk. There were unlikely to be camels,
for it seems very probable that the camel was not
domesticated before the end of the Bronze Age (about
1200 B.C.); nor were there horses, for these only
appeared in the Near East with the invasion of the
Hyksos (about 1800 B.C.).

While Terah's shepherds were putting the last touches
to their preparations for departure, the local farmers of
Ur went on with the tasks peculiar to the agricultural
civilization of Mesopotamia. In the fields adjacent to the
grassy plain peasants could be seen operating the heavy
sluice-gates which controlled the opening and closing
of the irrigation channels; the water running in these
channels was vital for the fertility of the crops — of the
wheat and barley especially.

It is hardly likely that anyone on this day, no different
from any other, paid attention to the small party of
shepherds setting out for a fresh camping ground. No
one spared a glance for the small tribe of nomads
surrounding the flocks of white sheep and black goats
as they went on their way. No one, it is certain, had any

idea that this tiny group already bore within it the spiritual destiny of a whole world.

Before we follow these nomads up the Euphrates on the journey along its banks for something like 800 miles, a journey which was to take them to the city of Haran in the Paddan-aram territory, we must endeavour to clarify our ideas on certain points on which the Bible is not very explicit.

Ur of the Chaldees

Abram was born in the region of Ur. In these surroundings he grew up and lived for many years before his departure for the land of Canaan, and this important Mesopotamian civilization must have left its stamp on Abram's mind, his manner of life and his psychology.

According to the Bible it does not appear that the Hebrews were ever very concerned about the exact topographical situation of Ur of the Chaldees,[3] which always remained a vague name, of no great interest. Yet it may well be that the name 'Hebrew', designating the men of Abram's tribe, signified 'the men from beyond the river', that is, 'the shepherds of the left bank of the Euphrates'.[4]

Ur, city of Sumeria
The Sumerians, the most surprising of men

Nowadays the ruins of Ur, in lower Mesopotamia, stand in the centre of an immense desert. All around the mound

[3] There is an anachronism here. The Chaldean invasion did not reach Mesopotamia until about 1100 B.C., seven centuries, therefore, *after* Abram. At the period when the scribe was writing this text (fifth century B.C.) the southern part of the Euphrates was known as Chaldea; this explains the error in the name.

[4] The ancient city of Ur (nowadays, al Mugayyar, the mountain of pitch) is situated on the *right* bank of the Euphrates. But photography has shown that in antiquity the course of the Euphrates certainly passed to the south of the city. At that time Ur was on the left bank of the river. Thus the Hebrews could unmistakably be called 'the tribe dwelling on the other bank of the river', at least by the people occupying the land of Canaan, that is, Palestine at the present day (see diagram, p. 152). According to certain orientalists the word Hebrew may well originate in the name of the patriarch Heber (or Eber), Abram's ancestor, mentioned in the genealogy (Gen. 11: 14). It may be added that the etymology of Hebrew in relation to the *Apiru* remains uncertain.

Abraham's clan camped on the left bank of the Euphrates, then had to cross over onto the right bank. This is how they came to be called 'Hebrews' ('men from beyond the river').

of ruins stretches bare sand under the burning sun. In Abram's day there stood here, in the delta of the Euphrates, a proud and powerful city, one of those city states with colossal religious architecture like others to be found on this immense plain: Uruk, Eridu, Lagash, Umma, Nippur, Adab (see map, pp. 12 and 13). Around these fortified sites stretched a rich countryside, perhaps even more luxuriant than the agricultural lands of the valley of the Nile.

This result was not secured without considerable effort, for unlike the valley of the Nile, flooding occurs here unexpectedly, and it is savage and devastating. If not properly canalized it carries all before it, houses and men, cattle and cultivation. Thus in this Mesopotamian region at the end of winter great labour is needed to prevent the catastrophic overflowing of the rivers. For this purpose, in the part of the country with which we are concerned, the Euphrates was confined, as if in a strait-jacket, between enormous earthen banks to prevent its flowing out over the neighbouring countryside. On the other hand, there could be no question of allowing these mud-laden waters to flow into the gulf, for the mud they bore was the agent of fertility; in addition they also provided the humidity which was indispensable for agriculture and indeed for life itself. Thus these waters of the annual flood had to be caught, stored in vast reservoirs and stocks of them built up. Afterwards, at will and as required for irrigation, their redistribution in the plain was effected by means of a complex system of canals, locks, channels and drains to transport fertility to the outlying districts.

This original form of agricultural planning was not carried out by the Semites. The men of Abram's race had nothing to do with the development of the land of Sumer, at any rate so far as its main life was concerned. The originators of this economic policy were the Sumerians, a people who preceded the arrival of the Semites in this land by more than 1500 years, as we shall see.

Where did the Sumerian tribes come from? Possibly their successive waves had the Asiatic provinces as their starting-point. Some authors are inclined to think that it was Afghanistan or Baluchistan, others that it was the Caucasus. In any case, at the end of the fifth millennium B.C., these hordes appear to have set out, and by the end of the fourth millennium (3500) we find them firmly established in the wide marshy plain formed by the deltas of the Euphrates and the Tigris.

The Sumerians belong neither to the Semitic branch

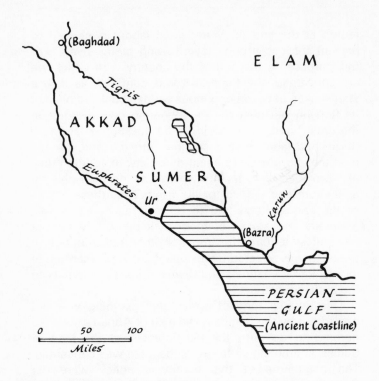

**VARIATIONS IN THE FINAL STAGES OF
THE COURSES OF THE GREAT
MESOPOTAMIAN RIVERS**

1. At the time of Abram (2nd millennium B.C.)

Notice the projection of the interior arm of the Persian Gulf which at that time penetrated some distance inland.

At the time of Abram the three great rivers (Karun, Tigris and Euphrates) flowed into the waters of the Persian Gulf by three separate estuaries.

It is well to point out here the site of the city of Ur (situated then at about 100 miles from the sea) on the left bank of the Euphrates. The Hebrew tribe of Abram, originating in the city-state of Ur, could, in consequence, be perfectly correctly designated by the phrase 'the people from beyond the river'.

VARIATIONS IN THE FINAL STAGES OF THE COURSES OF THE GREAT MESOPOTAMIAN RIVERS

2. At the present time

The dotted line shows the encroachment of the land over the sea. All this alluvial land has been brought down at the time of the great floods. Because of this Ur is situated nowadays some 225 miles from the coast.

In addition, owing to the change in the course of the river, the mound of Ur is at present situated on the right bank of the river. It will be noticed that the three rivers, which formerly had each its own mouth, now flow into the Persian Gulf through a delta common to them all.

N.B. For the sake of clarity these diagrams show only the city of Ur. For the general map of Sumer-Akkad, see pp. 12 and 13.

nor to the Aryan family. The extraordinary statue-portraits, full of vitality, which they have left us, indicate their ethnic type with startling realism. They were of medium height with low foreheads and prominent noses; their mouths were small and thin lipped and their chins unobtrusive. Their hair, which they wore very long, was separated by a parting. In ancient times they wore thick spade beards, often artificially waved. Later, they shaved the head and face.

After settling in this country which was henceforward known by their name (land of Sumer; the Bible calls it Shinar) these newcomers from the valley of the two rivers were to found a civilization of powerful originality; they built fortified cities; they used a pictographic form of writing at a period when the rest of humanity (except for the groups settled at this time in the valley of the Nile) was still at the stage of fumbling with polished stone. When, elsewhere, primitive peoples were painfully acquiring a rudimentary level of social life, the Sumerians built cities, put up colossal buildings and carved impressive funeral effigies.

From the political point of view the picture presented by Sumeria is less remarkable. All those isolated cities scattered about in lower Mesopotamia like pawns on a chessboard were a law to themselves; governed by self-interest, they thought only of increasing their own wealth. When the opportunity offered they did not hesitate to resort to force to impose their supremacy on neighbouring cities. As a result, the continual quarrels meant that the country was constantly at the mercy of fire and the sword. On different occasions all the wealthy cities of Sumer were destroyed, plundered, or burnt down, as the excavators have been able to discover. Over the ruins of civilizations thus razed to the ground by war another city was built which a little later was itself laid low; and so it continued. Even at the time of Abram, in about 1850 B.C., Ur appeared like an enormous citadel astride a hillock dominating the river and the plain. And it was the same with all the other Sumerian cities. These man-made hillocks are called *tells* by modern Arabs and the term has been adopted by the archaeologists.

Victory of the Semites of Akkad over the city-states of Sumer (about 2350 B.C.)

Towards the end of the third millennium, while Sumeria, an advanced centre of civilization, was weakened by wars between cities, a wave of invaders advanced insidiously from the North.

Whence came these warlike Semitic tribes who gradually made their way down the Tigris and Euphrates? Some historians have placed the origin of these nomads in Syria, others locate it in the Arabian peninsula. But it can be stated with certainty that after 3000 B.C. some of these invaders had started on the way to southern Mesopotamia. And soon, at the north of Sumer the Semitic kingdom of Akkad was established, compact and threatening, facing the divided principalities of Sumer. (See explanatory map, p. 26.) In about 2350 B.C. the Semitic sovereign of Akkad, Sargon I, called Sargon the Old, went to war against Sumer. His victory was complete, and so the kingdom of Akkad now stretched as far as the shores of the Persian Gulf. Together with the other cities of the delta, Ur – where five hundred years after these events Abram was to be born – was a dependency of the Semitic sovereign of Akkad whose palace and government were situated somewhere in the Babylonian region; his capital was Agade but its site has not yet been identified.

11

Mari

Anatu

Tut

THE GREAT URBAN CENTRES OF SUMER AND AKKAD

In about 3500 B.C. the Mesopotamian delta began to be occupied by Asiatic tribes who were neither Semites nor Aryans. The newcomers established themselves on the southern plain between the Tigris and the Euphrates. They were the founders of a very original civilization which, during the following centuries, was to develop successfully in Lower Mesopotamia. This was the period of the great independent city-states: Eridu, Uruk, Ur, Larsa, Lagash, Umma, Nippur, Adab, Isin etc.

In about 2500 waves of Semitic nomads began to arrive in Sumer; they came from the Arabian-Syrian regions by way of the middle Euphrates. They first settled at Mari. Shortly before 2350 Sargon founded the Semitic empire of Akkad (to the north-west of Sumeria). The site of Sargon's capital was Agade; this site has not yet been identified. Subsequently the wealthy, immense and magnificent Babylon was the capital of the State.

In about 2350 Sargon seized Sumeria. Sumeria and Akkad were united. The advanced civilization of Sumeria was to exert a great influence on the Akkadians.

It was within this curious and original Sumerian-Akkadian civilization that 500 years later the Semitic patriarch Abram was to be born (about 1900–1880 B.C.)

12

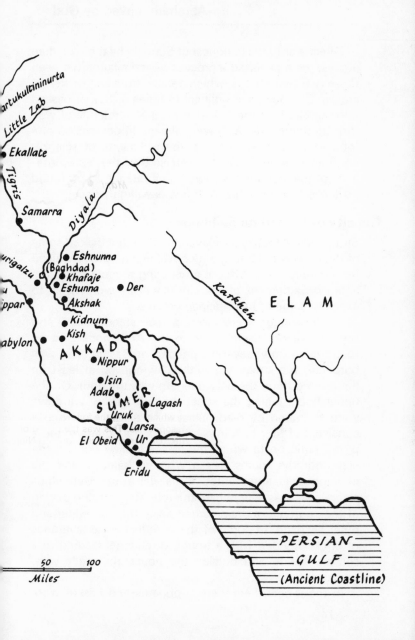

artukultininurta

Little Zab

Ekallate

Tigris

Samarra

Diyala

urigalzu

Eshnunna
(Baghdad)
Khafaje
Eshunna
Akshak

Der

Karkheh

ELAM

ippar

Kidnum

abylon

Kish

AKKAD

Nippur

Isin

Adab

SUMER

Lagash

Uruk

Larsa

El Obeid

Ur

Eridu

PERSIAN
GULF
(Ancient Coastline)

50   100
Miles

Directly after the conquest of Sumeria by the Akkadian armies, there occurred a process of assimilation between these two civilizations, which derived from such different stocks. Obviously the political fortunes of Sumer passed into the hands of the Akkadians – that is the rule of war. But the Sumerians, who were already in possession of a form of writing, an art, and the rudiments of science, continued, nonetheless, to exercise over the representatives of the 'occupying power' an influence as profound as it was incontestable. And it was willingly accepted.

The city of Ur and its buildings

Sir Leonard Woolley's excavations have uncovered some of the houses of Ur past which Abram must have walked from time to time. Without attempting to reconstruct the entire development of the city it will be worthwhile to examine some of its principal features.

The dwellings were more or less standardized, and bore a striking resemblance to the Arab houses to be found even nowadays in Baghdad or Basrah. The wall bordering the street was without windows, at least on the ground floor; the only opening was the door. On the upper floors facing the street the few narrow windows were shuttered by reed trellises. As a rule each house consisted of four buildings arranged in a square round a paved patio on to which the rooms looked out. On the first floor the rooms had a wooden balcony and the building was surmounted by a flat roof. Meticulous cleanliness was everywhere the rule. Beneath the paving of the courtyard a drain carried away the rain water and other seepage. In some of the corridors were lavatories of brick provided with a trough or channel leading to a soil-pit. Inside and outside the house the walls were whitewashed.

In the rooms there were cupboards and basket-work

chests. The beds, made of wood, were furnished with mattresses and quilts, often embellished with ornament of some kind. There were tables, seats and carpets. All this formed the setting for a comfortable and civilized life with, on occasion, a certain luxury.

In striking contrast with the interior cleanliness of the dwellings was the repellent filthiness of the narrow, winding and maze-like streets. Refuse collection did not exist — 'a filthy eastern city', is Sir Leonard Woolley's description.

At the centre of this city was the sacred area surrounded by a high wall, built in the shape of an oval of about two and a half miles in perimeter. On going inside, the Temenos, or sacred enclosure (400 yards long by 200 yards wide), which was easily recognizable, even at a distance, by its colossal, overwhelmingly massive architecture, one entered the special domain of the Moon-god

A ziggurat: an enormous construction of bricks from Sumer.

Nannar, the king and protector of the city-state of Ur.

Opposite the entrance to the Temenos stood twin temples. One was set apart for Nannar and his wife, the goddess Nin-Gal; the god was supposed to retire there during the day. The other building harboured the numerous secondary deities who formed the retinue of the royal couple.

Close to these buildings, overshadowing them, stood a huge tower, the ziggurat, whose general shape and history have both been discovered by the archaeologists. Abram must often have observed this ziggurat either from the plain where he pitched his tents or from within the sacred enclosure. For the son of Terah must have had to come here from time to time, to go to the temple of Nannar to carry out the ritual observances which certainly involved voluntary offerings, and possibly the obligatory payment of taxes.

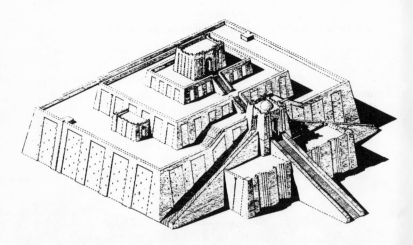

Reconstruction of the ziggurat at Ur.
(*Le monde d'Ur, d'Assur et de Babylon*, H. Schmöckel)

This colossal brick building, rectangular in shape, was three storeys high, each of them standing back on the one beneath so that the general appearance was that of a stepped pyramid. The base measured seventy yards in length by forty-six in breadth. The sides sloped slightly inwards and were strengthened by buttresses to resist the considerable lateral thrust.

A building of this sort must have contained millions of bricks. Some of them were merely dried in the sun and these were used for the inside walls. The others, baked in an oven, were used for the outside surfaces exposed to the sun, the wind and the rain. Slave labour and prisoners of war were certainly used in the construction of this huge mass.

Although not so wealthy as in times past, in Abram's time the city buzzed with activity. The weaving shops worked non-stop and in the port the loading and unloading of ships went on continuously. The streets were filled with a motley and noisy crowd.

In the quarter surrounding the sacred area, crowds of pilgrims made their way to the shrine, bringing with them the beasts that they came to offer to the Moon-god. Before the temples the priests of Nannar were busy receiving and recording all these gifts in kind offered to the god. The cellars of the Temenos were crammed with provisions which the scribes recorded carefully on bricks of soft clay; archaeologists have unearthed them from the sacerdotal archives. This would be the situation which influenced the young Abram early in the second millennium B.C.

Who was Abram?

There are three questions to answer here:

What was the social milieu in which Abram spent many years before leaving Sumeria?

To what branch of humanity did his family belong?
What was his race?

What exactly was the religion which by force of
circumstances Abram must have practised in the city of
the Moon-god until he set out for the land of Canaan?

Abram's social class at Ur

We know the distinctive characteristics of the social
system then in vogue at Abram's time in Sumeria.
Various legislative and administrative texts discovered
by the archaeologists furnish precise information on this
subject.

The three social classes in Abram's time (in about 1850 B.C.)

Next to the ruler (*patesi*), who was the god's representative, at the head of the hierarchy were the patricians or
amelu. To this category belonged the court dignitaries,
the high officials, the priests and the leaders of the army.

Immediately below this privileged class came the
mushkenu, the plebeians or free men; they were the
merchants, scribes and private individuals practising
liberal professions, landed proprietors and small farmers.

The third class was made up of the slaves, the *wardum*.
Among these were included prisoners of war, the children
of slaves and sometimes former free men reduced to
slavery by reason of debts that they were unable to pay.

With this in mind we can now inquire to which of these
three classes the patriarch Abram, a native of Ur and the
faithful subject of the Moon-god Nannar-Sin, belonged.
The Bible tells us nothing about this, but several
investigators have tried to provide an answer to the
question.

Abram's social class

According to certain theories Abram was quite simply a

'Chaldean' priest, that is, a wise man who in the peace of a religious atmosphere had assimilated all the knowledge of his times — mathematics, geometry, astronomy, geography, medicine, zoology and botany, philosophy and religion. Abram, then, would have formed one link in the long chain of the initiates trained through meditation on the Symbols and thereby enabled to attain to the heights of 'knowledge'.

All this belongs to the realm of fable. If Abram had been a learned man, a real fount of knowledge, or even merely a cultured man, the scribes of later times would not have failed, we may be sure, to record the fact as an important part of the tradition about the 'father of all believers'.

Abram was not a 'Chaldean' priest, well founded in Sumerian science (which was far from being a negligible quantity), nor a Babylonian initiate, well equipped with exotic and esoteric knowledge. Rather he was one of those perpetual wanderers in desert places, a man of open mind and keen intelligence, no doubt, but also, quite certainly, unable to read or to write cuneiform signs on a clay brick.

According to the British archaeologist, Sir Leonard Woolley, Abram, the townsman, left the city of Ur of his own free will. He left one of those houses whose site has been investigated by Woolley himself. In obedience to the orders of Terah, the head of the family, Abram, on this view, together with the whole of his household, left the city-state and set out for the steppe. This would fit in with the end of chapter 11 of Genesis, which tells us that: *Terah . . . made them leave Ur of the Chaldeans to go to the land of Canaan* (Gen. 11: 31). Woolley's theory, although it follows the biblical text scrupulously, seems to me, nevertheless, difficult to accept.

The truth is that it is inconsistent with the laws of

human geography: a nomad, sooner or later, is destined to settle down, but it is very unlikely that one who has done so will return to the life of a nomad.

Thus on psychological as well as on historical grounds it is difficult to imagine that Abram suddenly made up his mind purely and simply to desert his house at Ur with its rooms furnished with beds and cushions, his comfortable dwelling, cool in summer and warm in winter, his well-stocked cellar, his fountain of cool fresh water. It is inconceivable that a human being, especially one with a highly developed standard of life, should at one fell swoop reject all that to return to the nomadic civilization of his remote ancestors.

Moreover, even if the idea had entered the heads of Terah and his son Abram, to carry the plan into execution would have imposed great physical strains. To bear the severe conditions of wandering camp life, perpetually putting up and taking down the tents, to endure the exhausting tempo of this existence, a man must be born to it. The women and children, brought up in the city of Ur, would never have been able to survive so arduous an ordeal.

On the other hand, Abram could not have belonged to the official class, the *amelu*. In the first place the government would never have allowed his departure, for in the social system of that theocratic state it would have been equivalent to desertion. Add to this the fact that Abram's whole state of mind, which we shall shortly examine, was entirely at variance with a vocation to the life of an official or a warrior.

It is equally impossible to place him among the freed slaves. For how could a man of the slave class have amassed a sufficient sum to buy his freedom, together with that of his family, and become the leader of a pastoral tribe? So far we have only reached negative conclusions; a positive solution must now be attempted.

In the biblical text placed at the head of this chapter we are offered absolutely no information about Abram's social class during his time in Sumeria. Subsequently, however, the Old Testament, by implication, enlightens us on this point. Reading between the lines we observe a human group quite clearly adapted to the very special way of life to be found in nomadism. All the elements of this organization, comprising the leader, the shepherds, women, slaves, assume their very different roles rapidly and effectively. There is never any hitch in the planning of this work, despite its arduous nature. Nor is there any hesitation when an immediate decision is required by the unforeseen demands of life on the steppes or in the desert. Everything is carried out with the characteristic reactions of hardened nomads with a profound knowledge of their occupation and all its finer points, well able to deal with drought or the question of finding fresh pasture for their flocks.

And then it should be noticed that never once in Abram's time, in that of his grandson Jacob, or in the course of the first generations of his family, did any of them experience the least temptation to return to the life of the city. On the contrary, all the patriarchs and the men of their tribe showed considerable repugnance to an urban existence. They give the impression of deep attachment to a long-standing tradition as shepherds.

Consequently, when Abram and his father made up their minds to leave Ur, this small human group was not composed of city-dwellers, but of wandering shepherds, always on the move on the steppes. Abram was a wanderer, a nomad and the son of a nomad, whose ancestors for centuries past, possibly for a millennium or longer, had lived in tents. That seems the only conclusion.

Abram a Semite

Abram was a Semite; we have already encountered this term more than once. But such a term is valueless if unaccompanied by adequate explanation, and such an explanation is not always available.

Origin and evolution of the term Semite

The Semites, the Bible informs us, were the sons of Shem, who was himself the son of Noah.

The builder of the ark, it will be remembered, had three sons, Shem, Ham and Japheth. Like all the men of ancient times the Hebrews liked to think that a racial group must have a common ancestor. Thus Shem was regarded as the father of the Semites, Ham of the African peoples, the Canaanites and Egyptians, and Japheth of the men of white race (the Indo-European branch). Modern ethnology considers that the process of peopling the earth in general, and of the Near East in particular, was a matter of far greater complexity.

The genealogy of Shem is completed as follows. According to Hebrew tradition, amongst his descendants were Aram, Asshur and Eber, who became the 'fathers' of the three Semitic nations the Arameans, the Assyrians and the Hebrews.

Until the end of the eighteenth century this family notion of history was admitted without much discussion. Nevertheless, as the ethnologists, and, principally, the specialists in oriental languages, progressed in their researches it led to a gradual revision of the earlier thesis. And although agreement has not been reached between the various schools of thought it is possible to put forward the explanation which at the present time meets with the largest measure of acceptance.

No such thing as a Semitic race ?

Whether we are talking of Indo-Europeans or Semites,

of the black or yellow races, it would be futile at the present moment to seek in any country of the world what is customarily called a 'pure' race. Already in remote prehistorical times various human groups, with strongly contrasting characteristics, underwent considerable modification as a result of continual migration and inter-marriage. In addition, at the dawn of historical time (about 4000 B.C. for the Near East) in every place only populations of inextricably mixed ancestry are to be found.

As a matter of fact the Semites never constituted a distinct ethnic group. In prehistoric times, in northern Arabia we already find groups of wandering shepherds of differing origins and characteristics. They were tribes continually on the move, following their flocks. But, in the end, almost identical geographical and economic needs led these nomadic groups to adopt the same social customs, the same language, and the same ideas of legislation and coercion (*lex talionis*). Subsequently, there was mutual borrowing from one tribe to another of defensive religious rites and protective deities. By gradual stages all these elements, of very different character, came to present the same cultural appearance. There is, therefore, no Semitic race, but there is a Semitic civilization.

Better than a long explanation, diagrams showing the five great Semitic invasions (see p. 26 following) will enable the reader to follow the general progress of these tribes, and, more especially, the path followed by the Aramean group, to which Abram belonged.

Abram's religion at Ur

In the chapter of Genesis giving the life of Abram no information is given about the religion followed by Terah and his son Abram at the period when they dwelt at Ur in Sumeria. The only information that we have on this subject is to be found in a much later work, the Book of Joshua: *'In ancient days your ancestors lived beyond the River — such was Terah the father of Abraham and of Nahor — and they served other gods'* (Jos. 24: 2).

Teraphim of Tello.

Indeed for these wandering shepherds, always in quest of fresh grass and water, the fact of passing from the territory of one city-state to that of another, from the government of one prince to the dominion of a neighbouring *patesi* had, we may be sure, scarcely any importance. The itinerant Bedouin felt only a relative attachment to the great protective proprietary deity of the country (Nannar at Ur; Ianna at Uruk; Utu at Larsa, Enki at Eridu; and so on). They remained more readily attached to the old religious traditions of the former patriarchs of Arabia.

Thus the Semites of the second millennium revered certain gods who were given a marked personality, the sun and the moon, for example. In addition, they devoutly carried with them the *teraphim*, their little domestic idols; household gods who were the protectors of their families.

On the other hand, worship was paid to certain solitary trees, to caves and to springs, and to certain phenomena in connection with the atmosphere and the soil. All this enables us to understand that, on a final analysis, the authentic religious rites of the primitive peoples consisted not in prayers coming from the heart (a characteristic of religions in an advanced state of development) but in magic; by the help of the practice of sorcery, man, immersed in hostile surroundings, endeavoured to control external and invisible powers.

Such, on the whole, must have been the religious beliefs of Abram. It must be added that at the time when the small clan still dwelt 'on the other side of the river' its members looked on death as something different from annihilation. In Sheol, the dead continued to enjoy an existence similar to that which they had led on earth, but one with a slower tempo, and in an atmosphere that was far more dreary, and of course with no question of moral reward.

Finally, Abram must certainly have gone, at least on certain occasions, to the Temenos of Nannar, the Moon-god, to take part publicly, as one of the deity's subjects, in the sacrifices and obligatory ceremonies. On this account he must have had occasion to pass through some of the streets of the city of Ur, certain aspects of which have been described above.

It was in this curious spiritual ground that God was soon to plant his seed. It was ground ill prepared, it would seem, for the seed to germinate. How would the unenlightened mind of this ignorant Bedouin react to the call of God, to the summons of a supernatural being very different from what Abram could have hitherto known and venerated?

Reasons for the departure

Terah made them leave Ur of the Chaldaeans to go to the land of Canaan (Gen. 11: 31).

Why did they leave? Genesis offers no explanation. But there is no reason why we should not endeavour to discover the motive for this decision whose suddenness is foreshadowed by nothing in the biblical text.

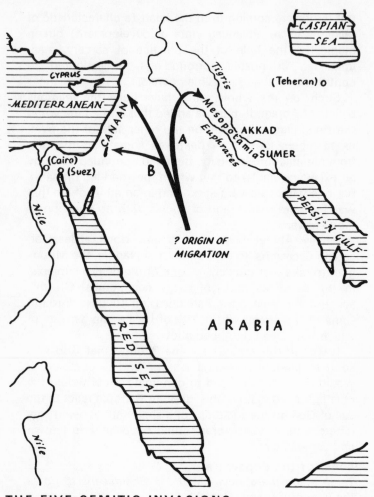

THE FIVE SEMITIC INVASIONS

In about 3000 B.C.

(a) A wave of warrior shepherds, coming from northern Arabia, settled in Mesopotamia (Akkadians).

(b) A second wave, from the same region, settled on the Mediterranean coast (the Amorites).

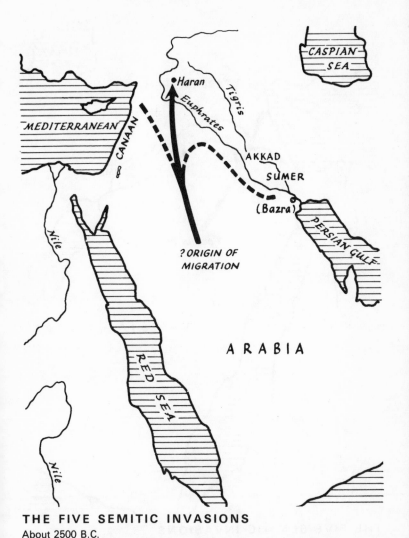

THE FIVE SEMITIC INVASIONS

About 2500 B.C.

(c) A second wave of Semitic shepherds, again from northern Arabia (the Arameans), settled in the Upper Euphrates and spread its small clans throughout the region (Abram). Later, in about 2000 B.C., these Arameans founded the kingdom of Damascus.

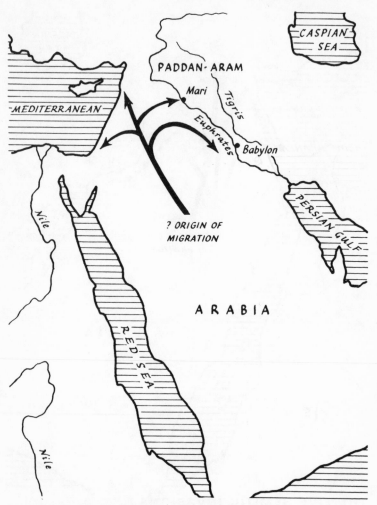

THE FIVE SEMITIC INVASIONS

    (d) A fourth wave of Semitic invaders — the Amorites, also from Arabia — fell upon the Near East: in the west they attacked Canaan, in the north Paddan-aram (Mari), in the east Babylon.

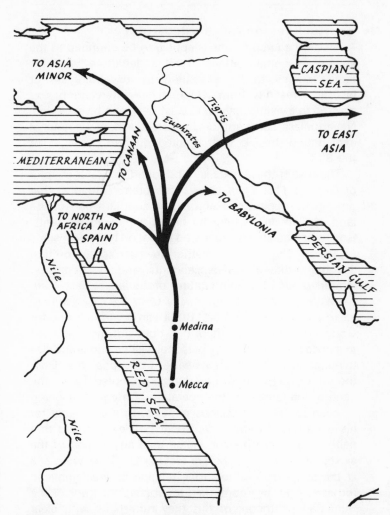

THE FIVE SEMITIC INVASIONS

(e) In the seventh and eighth centuries of our era there occurred the great invasion of the Mohammedan hordes who rapidly spread over the whole of the Near East, western Asia, North Africa and southern France (where Charles Martel brought them to a halt in 732).

No 'spiritual' reason for this departure

At Ur all the circumstances appear to be confined to the sphere of human affairs; Terah's departure with his family seems to be explained by psychological or historical reasons from which divine intervention, expressed in a visible manner at least, seems to be excluded. Nevertheless, some authors hesitate to accept the rational explanation, basing their opinion on two passages of the Bible.

The first of these texts is to be found in a later chapter of Genesis (15: 7). It shows us Abram, settled at that time in the region of Hebron (the southern part of the land of Canaan), where he had just pitched his tents. God, who had already appeared to him on three occasions (at Haran, Shechem and Bethel) revealed to him on that day the future of his descendants, and in conclusion reminded him of certain features of the recent past: *'I am Yahweh who brought you out of Ur of the Chaldeans to make you heir to this land.'* But it can be argued that for God to have 'brought them out' does not mean that on this occasion he did so by personal, visible and authoritative manifestation. It seems easier to suppose that God, the ruler of all men and all things, prompted Terah, the head of the family, by the operation of normal reasoning or even by a subconscious impulse, to make ready for his departure. In any case, it can be clearly stated that neither Terah nor his son Abram had any inkling of the existence of Yahweh before leaving Ur. They were still at the stage of the idolatrous religion of their nomadic forbears. And they continued to worship the gods of the Sumerian pantheon; of this they furnish us with clear proof. As followers of the Moon-god Nannar, both Terah and Abram chose the northern city of Haran as the objective of their lengthy migration, the only other Sumerian city placed, like Ur, under the invocation of

Nannar. If the two nomads, before leaving the lower Euphrates, had been influenced by the revelation and orders of Yahweh it is difficult to understand their taking so much trouble to remain under the protection of the Sumerian god.

The second text which causes a certain difficulty to some commentators occurs in the Acts of the Apostles. This passage describes the appearance of Stephen, the first Christian martyr, before the high priest and the Sanhedrin, who were to condemn him. In putting forward his defence Stephen declared that the *God of glory appeared to our father Abraham, when he was in Mesopotamia,* before he lived in Haran, *and said to him, 'Depart from your land and from your kindred and go into the land which I will show you.'* Then he departed from the land of the Chaldeans and lived in Haran (Acts 7: 2, 3).

Before the Jewish tribunal which, he was well aware, was shortly to sentence him to be stoned as a 'blasphemer', Stephen spoke as an advocate, a confessor of the faith and a zealous preacher. He cannot be blamed for not speaking as a careful historian. He was recounting an event which happened nearly two thousand years beforehand. We must not hold him too closely to an interpretation which is possibly the echo of a late Jewish tradition.

In conclusion, it appears that there is no need to invoke a supernatural explanation for this departure. At Ur, God gave no clearly expressed order. We must look, rather, to psychological and historical reasons.

The real motive for departure

The real motive for departure is furnished by history in general and social history in particular.

Terah's family lived during the social confusion of Sumeria on its conquest by Akkad at the beginning of the nineteenth century B.C., so something must be said to begin with about the political situation of the southern region of Mesopotamia. The third dynasty of Ur, whose advanced civilization had shone brilliantly, had just fallen in 1955 B.C. to the onslaught of a Semitic conqueror who established the capital of his kingdom at Isin. Now at Larsa, some ninety miles distant, there was a rival dynasty (also Semitic) rising threateningly against the sovereign of Isin. These two States were at war for two hundred years (1955–1755); sometimes the cities of the former Sumeria depended on Larsa, sometimes they gave obedience to Isin. For this reason the long period is called by orientalists the Isin-Larsa period. In passing it may be noted that the youth and departure of Abram occurred during this troubled period of prolonged hostilities.

Thus the Semites proved the uncontested masters of Mesopotamia. Logically the clan of Terah, encamped near Ur, should have been perfectly satisfied with this political situation, since they were among men of their own stock.

In fact, settled residents, whether city-dwellers or farmers, have little liking for nomads on the fringe of a well established State organization. From inscriptions on clay bricks we know that the inhabitants of the cities referred to these perpetual wanderers as 'brigands and cut-throats' and other similar names.

Disliked by all (including their own race, as we have seen), deemed undesirable by the governments (even Semitic governments) and cordially hated by the established population, these wandering shepherds themselves decided to leave the inhospitable lands of the kingdoms of Babylon. They knew where they were to go, as the Bible tells us: *Terah made them leave Ur . . . to go to the land of Canaan.* Why did they go there? It was because they knew that vast open spaces were to be found in this Mediterranean land near the other end of the Fertile Crescent. The grass there was sufficient for their flocks, there were few cities, and they could wander untroubled. At the time of Abram the regions at the south of Canaan were under the dominion of Egypt, a remote sovereignty, very gentle and almost slack in operation. In Babylon, Terah and all the Aramean shepherds, his brothers, had to bear the rule of a totalitarian, theocratic State, whereas to the south-west of the Jordan there was, it seemed, a country ruled by an easy-going government. There would be no more scribes with their figures and statistics, no more tax collectors! There was complete freedom to wander and an ideal isolation. Terah and his people, retiring like all nomads, chose freedom.

Cuneiform tablets, the result of excavations in Babylon, reveal by implication at least that the departure of Terah's clan must not be considered as an isolated historical event. Throughout the whole of the first half of the second millennium there was a general exodus of these Aramean shepherds towards the north-west. Some groups went to settle in the region that is now called Syria. Others migrated to Transjordania (to the east of Jordan and the Dead Sea), or again to Canaan (now Palestine). Some clans even pressed on to the eastern borders of the Nile delta where the Egyptian officials granted them permission to settle on the fringes of the cultivated land and the desert. It was a departure en masse, the great Aramean migration.

2

HARAN: GOD SPEAKS TO ABRAM

Ur to Haran represented a journey of something like eight hundred miles, if the many necessary detours are included. The eight hundred miles were covered at the slow pace of the sheep which, as they went along, were continually stopping to crop the grass that was often dried up by the sun. But, as always in the East, there was no hurry.

The Clan of Terah

Genesis gives us the names of the head of the clan and the members of the family. The patriarch was called Terah. He had three sons: Abram, Nahor and Haran. Haran, who died at Ur before the departure of the caravan, left a son, Lot, on whom devolved an important ethnic role. Nahor seems to have remained for the time being at Ur; it was only later on that he left Sumeria (see Genealogical table, page 35).

Abram was accompanied by his wife, Sarai, who was his half-sister; she was, in fact, Terah's daughter but not by the same mother as Abram. According to the Sumero-Akkadian law, such a union was regarded as perfectly lawful. It was a small, in fact, a very unpretentious clan of nomads, more than a family though not yet a tribe. Some explanation is needed here.

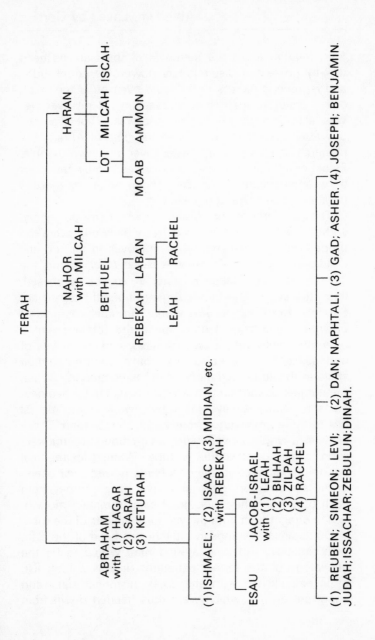

In relation to all the members of the clan, its head usually possessed discretionary power. He could judge and reprove; if necessary he could even order the death of his children, his grandchildren and his relatives. He was also free to sell them as slaves. That was the unwritten law of the desert. At the time of Abram, the patriarch reigned as a master over his own people. Evidence of this is to be found when, under the most tragic circumstances, we see Abram about to make a ritual sacrifice of his son Isaac.

The wife, and on occasions, the wives (for polygamy, without being obligatory, was freely allowed), were the property of the husband, who, moreover, in the day-to-day language of the family was called *ba'al*, that is, the master. The wife, taken prisoner in war or purchased, had little say in the family organization of the ancient Semites. Her function was work. The legal customs of polygamy and concubinage made the formation of a powerful family unit a swift process, and the slaves of both sexes, who were also very prolific, contributed their share to the continued increase of the community. When the number of sons grew too large, they then formed new clans, remaining always united by very close sentimental ties to the ethnic source from which they sprang. These clans as a whole, all venerating a common ancestor, very soon came to constitute a tribe. When geographical conditions allowed it, the shepherds grazed their sheep in the same region, often at several days' journey from each other; but they took good care to remain more or less in direct touch with the various elements of the tribe.

On summer evenings in the tent, the head of the clan, with the men squatting around him, would recite the genealogy of the former patriarchs. It was a long list, often embellished with anecdotes, historical feats, and important events, which were thus handed down from

36

generation to generation in a set form which soon became unchangeable. It is easy to understand how this oral tradition came to possess a very marked character of authenticity.

Does this mean that all the clans of the same tribe were descendants of the same ancestor? The Semites held this to be the case. In reality, from time to time each of these primitive clans were joined by other small groups encountered by chance in their wanderings on the steppes. Both parties weighed the advantages of joining forces. Then a very simple symbolic ceremony took place: the two chiefs, as representatives of the two clans, opened a vein of their arms and exchanged blood; and so the strangers became an integral part of the large family, they were now of the same blood as all the natural descendants of the ancestors.

Henceforward, the members of an ethnic group (at the simplest stage a clan, at the most developed stage, a tribe) regarded themselves as members of one body. An insult to one of them became an offence experienced by all. If the blood of an individual member of the clan or tribe was shed, the report spread at once among the shepherds belonging to the same family group and the cry went up 'our blood has been shed!' And so it can be understood how these men of the steppes were inspired by a collective feeling of vengeance, or 'vendetta'.

The sons and grandsons of the patriarch, the wives and concubines of the chief, the servants of the wives, and the tribal elements artificially associated by the rite of exchange of blood all formed the various constituent elements of the clan. To these must be added the servants and the slaves.

Physical appearance of Abram's clan

By an extraordinary chance, we are able to have a fairly

37

clear idea of the physical appearance of Abram and the members of his clan. In an Egyptian tomb, sumptuously arranged to harbour the mummy of the governor Chnumhotep, archaeologists have discovered a wall-painting in brilliant colours, representing a group of thirty-seven Semite nomads who were contemporaries of the patriarch Abram. This is extremely valuable evidence for those concerned with biblical history.

This wall-painting at Beni-hasan (the modern name of the village in which the tomb of Chnumhotep was discovered) can be dated with certainty; in a corner of the picture an Egyptian is brandishing a sheet of papyrus giving all the necessary information about the period in which this mural was painted. It was the sixth year of Pharaoh Sesostris II (twelfth dynasty), that is the year 1901 (or 1898, according to certain authors) B.C.

If we accept the date of 1850 for the adult age of Abram, the work of art in question would therefore be scarcely fifty years earlier than what is known as the religious period of the patriarch. Within a few years, it

Wall painting from Beni-has

could be contemporary with his youth. These Amorites, pictured at Beni-hasan, belonged to a branch which was a neighbour of the one to which Abram belonged. Both Amorites and Arameans for long led a similar pastoral existence; it is well known that this kind of life on the steppes stamps an individual in the same way as living in a settled community does.

A closer examination of this work reveals the sheik at the head of the procession, and the hieroglyphs give his name as Chief Ibsha (a genuine Semitic name). His finely chiselled features are characteristic of his race. His thick black hair is trimmed to cover his head like a cap and his almond-shaped eye, sparkling with malice and intelligence, peers out under a prominent brow. His upper lip is shaven, but a fine beard traces a thin line along his jaw, coming to a small elegant point beneath his chin. Ibsha and his companions are dressed in clothes of various kinds: some of them, the torso bare, wear a fairly long loin-cloth reaching from the waist to the knees; the men-at-arms, with their lances and bows, wear robes

Abram and his family must have looked like this group of Bedouins

leaving either the right or the left shoulder bare. On the backs of the donkeys accompanying the retinue other arms, javelins, bows and staves, are carefully packed together.

With a resolute air the women, clad in multi-coloured tunics, push forward in a group. They are well-built, sturdy matrons, with large busts, admirably suited for motherhood. Beautiful black hair falls down to their shoulders and in pigtails over their chests. According to this wall-painting, therefore, we have clear evidence that in Abram's time the women were not veiled; we see them here, their faces free to the air with no fear of showing themselves. This enables us to observe how the Semitic type is more marked in the female sex: large, beautiful eyes but also a more pronounced nose, a certain heaviness of features and a general appearance of plumpness. The Egyptian artists, who could seize on the slightest picturesque detail with no attempt at caricature, have put on record a series of accurate sketches.

An inscription informs us of the trade of these foreigners: 'arrival of the black paint for the eyes brought by the thirty-seven Asiatics'. It refers, in fact, to cosmetics intended for the women of the valley of the Nile. The Semites whom we see here could not, therefore, be regarded merely as shepherds; nonetheless, they were nomads living, like all the shepherds of Terah and Abram, in tents.

Thus, with no forcing of words and taking care not to exceed the rights of a commentator on a work of art, we may well believe that the wall-painting at Beni-hasan provides us with a very close idea of the physical appearance of Terah's small nomadic clan.

n the road from Ur to Haran

To go right across Babylon might well appear a some-what dangerous undertaking for nomads, and, indeed,

almost impossible of realization on account of the topo-
graphy. For in this rich countryside situated between the
two rivers stood busy cities, farms and vast expanses of
cultivated land. At each step canals would be encountered, and although some of them were no wider than a
large ditch, others resembled real rivers. It was an
aquatic network with numerous tentacles, an insuperable
obstacle for a band of shepherds encumbered with
baggage and followed by their flocks. It can be inferred,
therefore, that the Hebrew clan preferred to go up the
Euphrates along its western bank, adjacent to the desert,
taking care, so far as possible, to keep clear of the urban
centres.

As it went on its way the caravan would certainly see
in the distance the lofty ziggurat of Babylon, the
'Mountain of God' or 'the hill of heaven', an enormous
building rising to upwards of 180 feet above the vast
plain in which palm forests and fields of cereals rippled
in the breeze like the waves of a great sea. All along the
river they could admire the little inland ports spaced out
near the great commercial centres and the Bedouin
camping sites. They must surely have passed in sight of
the fine red ziggurat of Mari, an arrogantly wealthy city
which, at that date, had no more than a hundred years
to live.

They had to keep moving. They had not yet reached
the principal stage of their journey. Here they were at
Deir (Der, El-Der), a business and agricultural centre, the
economic hub of the region. Then came Zelibi, the former
Zenobia, perched on a rock which the lines of caravans
passed coming from Palmyra and going on towards
Persia. Finally in the neighbourhood of the Nahr-Belik
(a tributary of the Euphrates) they came to Rakka, which
much later was to become the capital city of the powerful
caliph Haroun al-Raschid, Charlemagne's contemporary.

In all this region there were fords which enabled men and beasts to cross the river. Thus it was that, after a lengthy journey and, also, most certainly, after heavy trials, Terah's clan made their way up the Kara (a tributary of the Nahr-Belik) on the eastern bank of which stood the city of Haran in Upper Mesopotamia.

Haran, where God spoke to Abram

But on arrival in Haran they settled there (Gen. 11: 31). Nowadays the tiny village of Haran (the biblical name has hardly changed) is a group of whitewashed houses, each of which is surmounted by a conical roof like a bee-hive. It is a wretched little place.

Behind the village is the tell formed by the various brick-built cities which stood on this site; in succession they crumbled one on the other, generally as a result of wars. The high crest of this artificial hill gives us an idea of the importance of the city of Haran in ancient times; it was one of the most frequented centres of this land known as Aram-Naharaiim (Aram of the two rivers) or Paddan-aram, literally the 'plain of Aram', or rather the 'road of Aram', which emphasizes the character of this region as a highway.

Haran, an Aramean pastoral centre

Terah's clan had good reason to make a prolonged stay in Haran. In the first place, it was important, after the arduous journey from Ur to Haran, to allow their flocks to recover by a long rest with good pasture. Losses in animals must have been appreciable. Before setting out on the further 700 mile journey (the distance approximately from Haran to the south of the Land of Canaan) they would need to restock their herds by natural means. That would require several years for ewes normally drop only one lamb each spring.

It may be noted in passing that Terah and his clan can

scarcely have felt themselves out of their element in Paddan-aram. In the pasture lands near Haran they could still feel at home, for they continued to be under the protection of Nannar-Sin, the Moon-god of Ur. The choice of the Haran region, the only one in northern Mesopotamia placed under the heavenly protection of Nannar, cannot therefore be regarded as the result of mere chance.

It should be emphasized, moreover, that Terah and Abram, as Arameans, found themselves in good company in the Paddan-aram region. It seems indeed that at this period groups of Aramean nomads (to use biblical language) had settled here and there throughout the whole region of Haran. These wandering shepherds seemed to creep in everywhere. From the delta of the Euphrates to the upper reaches of the two rivers on the steppes at least, these little clans of Aramean[1] shepherds were to be found at every turn. But in the heighbourhood of Haran the Aramean ethnic element was largely in the majority, and we know that in this province the Aramean language remained in use for some time. In addition, worship of the Aramean deities was maintained for centuries to come.

When Abram arrived in sight of Haran he would have observed, at the foot of the fortress, a city with houses surmounted (as still is the case today) by roofs in the form of a sugar-loaf. It was an extraordinary form of architecture, effected by placing bricks one upon another, but not bound together by cement. This was because of the deficiency of wood, for not a single tree is to be found in this region.

Abram would not have actually lived in Haran, any more than he had lived in the city of Ur. From time to

[1] The Aramean nomads were not then established as an historical group, as they were to become later in about 1000 B.C.

Buildings of town-dwellers, at Haran

time he must have gone into the city to sell wool or buy corn and salt, but he and his shepherds would normally find themselves fully occupied with their flocks: animals to be cared for or to be moved to fresh pasture. Between Haran and the nearby course of the Euphrates stretches the plain of Servdj (its modern name) surrounded by a circle of hills whose lower slopes come to an end on the steep banks of the river. It is a small enclave, scarcely twelve square miles in area, furrowed with little streams in the rainy season, in which some twenty villages are to be found. Quite certainly Abram and his shepherds with their sheep must have traversed the length and breadth of this small area.

Near the present village of Haran is the well to which the village women and the wives of the nomads come even nowadays, morning and evening, to fetch their

45

water; it provides a golden opportunity for gossiping. Near the curb are the earthenware troughs, to which the shepherds lead their flocks at the close of the day. It is very probable that this same well was used by Abram's shepherds. [2]

Abram becomes head of the clan

Terah's life lasted two hundred and five years; then he died at Haran (Gen. 11 : 32).

It may be well here to say a word on the question of the longevity of the patriarchs, whose ages, it will be noticed, decrease as we get nearer to historical times. Anthropologists who have specialized in the study of human remains consider that the duration of human life has scarcely changed for thousands of years past. How, then, are we to explain the astonishing figures given in the Bible? The explanation is simple enough. At the period with which we are concerned, long life was regarded in the East as a special blessing granted to the righteous. If therefore a man reached an advanced age it must be because he was a righteous man, so these high figures had a symbolic meaning.

An important stage in this story is reached with the death of Terah and the inheritance by Abram of the leadership of the small clan of nomads. The head of the clan among the nomad Semites possessed something more than the ordinary authority of a leader; since he was responsible for economic and military policy he was regarded as endowed with genuine supernatural powers.

[2] The wells of these semi-desert regions must not be thought of as like our modern wells which are narrow and deep with a raised curb. The wells of the Near East have a diameter at their opening of eight to twelve feet, thus enabling a fair number of shepherds to draw water at the same time. Obviously, the depth depends on the underground water level. Usually the well is surrounded by large rough stones to a height of between one and a half to two and a half feet above the ground to prevent the caving in of the sides. Over the centuries these stones have been worn into a series of parallel ridges by the rubbing of the cords pulling up the filled buckets.

In case of need, he was able to command the sun, the moon, and even, in time of persistent drought, the clouds — or at least so all his own people firmly believed. These magic powers of the head of the nomad shepherds foreshadow, it seems, the appearance among the tribes of the priest-kings of the East, and even, at a very much later date in the West, the belief in the divine right of kings, on the model of Louis XIV of France, for example.

And here, too, we can perceive the origin of the sceptre which later on David, Solomon and many other ancient and modern sovereigns hold in their right hands when seated hieratically on their thrones. Quite simply, it was originally the shepherd's staff, the crook, the insignia of the head of the clan. The bishop's crozier clearly shows this origin. With the Semite nomads the staff was the symbol of government (cf. Gen. 49: 10; Judg. 5: 14) just as it is for field marshalls in some countries. The meaning of the symbol was well known to all, as is proved by the fact that in the Hebrew language the same term *shebet* signified both 'tribe' and 'staff'.

The baton which the Semitic chief held in his hand was also believed to have magical powers. At the height of the Israelite period we find the chiefs 'digging wells', that is, finding the subterranean water level which was necessary for the subsistence of the men and the flocks, using their staffs, probably, as sorcerer's wands (Num. 21: 16–18).

Thus on the day that Terah died his oldest son, his heir, Abram, assumed the chief's staff.

Yahweh said to Abram (Gen. 12: 1)

Suddenly an unknown, powerful God, of whom no one hitherto had the slightest idea, 'revealed himself to Abram'. He spoke to him and ordered him to leave Haran, but was silent about the precise country to which the patriarch was finally to direct his steps.

The Bible relates this first contact between Yahweh and Abram with somewhat disconcerting abruptness. In all its simplicity, of course, the account bears the marks of a most impressive occurrence. The condensed style of the passage is evidence that the writer of this chapter regarded this episode as a religious and national tradition which it was sufficient to refer to in a few words. Historians of the twentieth century A.D., always concerned to place an action or an event within its social and spiritual setting, in the circumstances require far more detail than the Israelite in ancient Palestine. Of course, with the valuable help of subsequent chapters of the Bible itself, and also in the light of the history of religions, we shall be able at least to obtain more light upon the subject, even though it is impossible to reconstruct all the circumstances of this interview between God and Abram.

On several occasions the Bible reports conversations between Yahweh and the patriarchs; this is the moment, perhaps, to examine under what form these manifestations of the Most High took place.

There is an obvious parallel here with the experiences Christians have had of conversations with our Lord Jesus Christ throughout the centuries, from the encounter of St Paul on the Damascus Road right through to our own times. But it should be made clear at the outset that according to the theologians, and also the great mystics, appearances of Christ must be considered extremely rare manifestations.

As regards the appearances of Yahweh to Abraham, the most general explanation is that God spoke to the patriarch (and later to his sons and afterwards to the prophets) by an interior language reaching their mind directly. Are we then to regard all these visions as taking place, always and exclusively, solely in the mind of the recipient? Not entirely, for it may well be that on exceptional occasions some external vision, affecting the senses, did occur; manifestations of this kind would constitute genuine appearances.

This revelation, this formidable spiritual revolution which, whether we like it or not, has so influenced the whole of the moral and social organization of our western civilization, can be summed up in a few words. It was the proclamation of the one, the only God; the proclamation of a holy God; and the progressive establishment of a moral law enabling man to attain to an ever loftier and purer form of morality. Of this threefold affirmation Abram's contemporaries could have, of course, not the slightest idea. We must now consider shortly the significance of this imposing message.

One God

One God: such an idea at that time, in the ancient world, was absolutely unthinkable. Elsewhere, in the Near East, as in the other neighbouring countries and even in other continents, the most clearly marked form of polytheism prevailed. Hindus, Sumerians, the Semites of Arabia, Babylon and Canaan, the Egyptians, the peoples of Africa or Asia, the remote civilizations of America; in those far off times, everywhere men invoked an infinite plurality of gods. For them a tree was a god, a raised stone was the dwelling place of a god, as was a mountain, a river and the sea. Similarly, the wind, clouds, lightning, and of course the earth itself and each star were gods. 'Everything was god, except God,' as Bossuet remarks.

And now to this shepherd, ignorant and an idolater, entirely lacking in any theological knowledge, suddenly there was revealed, without any preparation it appears, a God who insists on being the only one. Nowadays, nearly four thousand years after Abram, this idea of God is one with which we are familiar. But at the time of the patriarch it was an absolutely incomprehensible notion, inaccessible to the human mind. We have only to consider the facts: nearly five thousand gods in Babylon, thousands of them, also, in Egypt. The Semites, confirmed polytheists, had a fine collection of idols, fixed or portable, which were carved and made the object of worship. We find colleges of priests, who tried to bring order to this complexity by establishing a hierarchy, so far as they could, among the numerous elements of the pantheons. And so in certain regions, even in certain cities, preponderant influence was attributed to one god or another. But nowhere was it a question of one only god; it meant merely that one god was, as it were, promoted from among the others, which remained as numerous as before. Of course, religious evolution, and still more invasion, constantly produced radical changes in this mythological system of gods. It was a list under continual process of revision. At the same time other popular gods arose, here and there, as if to increase the theological confusion.

It is certainly difficult for us, with our modern outlook, in which the idea of one sole God is the only acceptable one, to obtain a clear idea of this 'metaphysical leap' represented by the revelation made to Abram and its acceptance by him. Here we may see the first sign, no matter how small it may be, of the realization that the god of the Hebrews is the one true God. Henceforward a real gulf separated the patriarch from his contemporaries, including the advanced priests of Egypt or Sumeria.

A holy God

If we look at the religions of the Near East (though it was just the same at this period in all parts of the world) we cannot suppress a certain feeling of disgust at all these deities of Sumer, Akkad and Egypt, where all is material- istic, sensual and immoral. The gods are married, they have children who are disrespectful, to say the least. Adultery, incest, murder, parricide and untruth prevail. These so-called 'supernatural' beings, who reign over mankind, are inspired by the most degrading passions, and during their meetings, which on occasion are more like orgies, they carouse, get drunk, and plot the most perverse activities imaginable.

Since all the inhabitants of these lofty spheres were powerful, man's especial concern was to prevent their harming him. And so there were the sacrifices of animals before the altar. A bargain was struck: a man offered an ox, and in return the god spared him some trial. This act of magic had no other end than to constrain the god to bow to his request; there was no compunction of heart; and remorse, or love, were sentiments that were hardly known. Religion was reduced on a final analysis to rites demanding the shedding of blood, and to ritual crimes. In certain temples sacred prostitutes were to be found who gave themselves to visitors, and also male prosti- tutes, who were held, of course, to be no less sacred. It was all very primitive, but no one was unduly concerned about it.

And then, suddenly, at Haran God spoke to Abram. As historians we too can recognize the presence of this God, the God of Abraham, by looking at the moral work which he accomplished in this man, in the clan, and in the people whom he chose. And he appeared absolutely alone; as a general rule he is absolutely invisible to his faithful followers; as a pure spirit he exacts a spiritual worship, adoration in spirit; he is a holy God.

It is possible to find in the Old Testament certain anthropomorphic characteristics which seem to clash with the notion of holiness. Yahweh in the Bible appears on occasion to be carried away by anger, he talks of vengeance, he says that he repents for acting in some way or another. Yet we must not forget that we are dealing with the origins of the Chosen People, and so we must not be too severe on those who took part in these episodes or recounted them; these wandering shepherds had not yet been able to free themselves entirely from the polytheism, both Semitic and Sumerian, with which they had been imbued for thousands of years past.

One only God. It was a matter for the time being, of course, of the 'only God of the clan of Abram', a tribal God, the protector of this small group of nomads. Five centuries later, on Sinai, we reach a further spiritual stage: Yahweh, always the only God, was there accepted as the God of Israel. He is a national God. After this, on the ground thus prepared, in the eighth and seventh centuries, arose the monotheism of the great prophets, and then, in the last place, Jesus, who tore down the veil of the temple, proclaimed that the Father is the only God, is supranational, the God of all men.

These three stages show us clearly the 'progressive' nature of the Old Testament. We must not expect too much of Abram. Even if his God is still only the God of his clan he remains nonetheless the one and only God. That is the essential fact and it is an extraordinary novelty in the history of religions, the remarkably fruitful contribution of this small Hebrew clan to the mind and heart of man. So we must not expect too much of Abram, the Hebrew shepherd, but rather consider the very great difficulties experienced by the men of this 'religious prehistory' in accepting, understanding and describing such novel ideas.

Nor must we forget the essentially concrete nature of

the ancient Hebrew language; it can only suggest abstract ideas by means of images and symbolism; that is its beauty as well as its weakness. It can only describe the nature and attributes of God by using terms that apply to man; as a result there are certain anthropomorphic features which can disturb the reader. But the faithful Jew made no mistake about it. *'For I am God',* declared Yahweh, *'not man'* (Hosea 11: 9).

A progressive religion

The elements of pagan religions are essentially static: nothing in them encourages evolution towards an increasingly lofty moral idea, however much desired or however desirable. When ancient religions developed in any way they owed their evolution to codifications carried out by the priests, to the fancies of the popular imagination and, most of all, to the influence of neighbouring nations. From this resulted in some cases a theological development which is easily explicable on historical grounds.

Nothing comparable occurred in Abram's religious experience. His jealous attachment to his one God, a God of justice and purity, enabled the Hebrew to set out on the path leading to an ever nobler moral, religious and social life. That is not to say that from time to time falls did not occur, as we shall have occasion to observe. But each time Yahweh's faithful people rose again, increased in stature by their remorse, with a clearer idea of their duty and a burning desire to go higher still. This thirst for hope and diligence in the pursuit of virtue will be sought for in vain among the pantheist mythologies of the ancient world. Such spiritual dynamism only existed in Israel and constituted the internal strength, originality and spiritual power of the Chosen People. All the great materialist empires which, down the course of history, seemed to crush and annihilate Israel, have perished. They have literally been reduced to ruins. Many of them have fallen to dust and knowledge of their existence has only come through the archaeologist's spade and the lens of the decipherer of manuscripts, and yet the soul of so tiny a people as Israel still lives. Indeed the idea of moral perfectibility, which is the very basis of the religion of Abram, has borne fruit in the western world, and influences it at every moment (modern social laws are but its living continuation); and it never ceases to produce new developments for the future.

The name of Abram's God

The God who revealed himself to Abram is frequently designated in the Book of Genesis by the term 'Yahweh'. In Exodus we are told how God for the first time revealed his name of Yahweh to Moses on Mount Sinai (Exod. 3: 13–15). This occurred in about 1230 B.C. As was mentioned above, Abram's period was in about 1850. Since Abram lived more than six hundred years before Moses he cannot have known the name Yahweh. And yet this name crops up continually in the story of the patriarch. This apparent contradiction arose from the way in which the stories reached the written form in which we now have them.

It is important to have a clear idea of how the Pentateuch was formed from the primitive compositions. [3] The following resumé traces the formative process of the first five books of the Bible, which were the works of

---

[3] The Pentateuch, or the Five Books, known by the Israelites as the Law or Torah, is made up, as the name indicates, of five parts. 1. *Genesis,* in which after a brief cosmogony we have the religious prehistory and proto-history. 2. *Exodus,* beginning with the flight from Egypt of the sons of Israel under the leadership of Moses. 3. *Leviticus* in which are the laws of the priests of the tribe of Levi. 4. *Numbers,* in which the census of the tribes is described. 5. *Deuteronomy,* or the 'Second Law'.

several collaborators. Historians nowadays are almost unanimous in recognizing three successive stages in the development of the text of the Pentateuch.

The first stage consists of the early 'history' of the clan and then of the Hebrew tribes, which was first preserved in oral form. On summer evenings the chief, or some story teller with a sonorous voice, recited in an unchanging, stereotyped form the adventures and exploits of famous ancestors. It is well known that in the East, even nowadays, these traditions are handed down from one generation to another in a fixed verbal form.

In the second stage these accounts, regarded as sacred, were carefully transmitted by word of mouth, and sometimes also in writing, in the circles of priests or scholars attached to certain sanctuaries.

The third and last stage was when the various cycles current in different places were gathered together to form the text of the Pentateuch as it has come down to us today.

'Various cycles' were mentioned in the last paragraph. Hebrew scholars, by examination of the vocabulary and the literary genre peculiar to each, have succeeded in discovering and separating four different compositions. Each of these four versions was composed at different periods. They are distinguished by the following names:

The *Yahwistic* tradition. In this account, for the divine name the author almost exclusively uses the name Yahweh. It is a vivid, colourful narrative, popular in conception and forcefully told. It seems to have originated in the south (kingdom of Judah) and the approximate date of this final version is that of the reign of Solomon (970–935 B.C.). Biblical historians designate this tradition by the letter J (Yahweh).

The *Elohistic* tradition (known as the E tradition by the exegetes) is so called because in this text God is designated by the name of Elohim.[4] This account was drawn up in the north of Palestine (the kingdom of Israel) at a slightly more recent period, it seems, than the Yahwistic tradition. It has a more sober, lofty moral style, and as Fr Roland de Vaux remarks 'is concerned to mark a sharper distinction between God and man'.

Then there is the *Priestly* cycle. Whereas the Yahwistic and Elohistic cycles do not concern themselves with legislative matters, the priestly tradition lays special stress on precise statement of the law regarding the organization of the sanctuary, festivals and sacrifices, and everything to do with ritual. Even the narrative portions betray a legalistic spirit. The style is abstract and rather formal. It is thought that a beginning was made with the collection of materials for the work during the Babylonic captivity (587–538); the definitive version followed shortly afterwards on the return to Palestine. Historians consider that the cycle was the work of the priests of the temple of Jerusalem; hence the letter P.

Lastly, there is the *Deuteronomic* tradition, which was preserved by the prophets; it has a somewhat halting style with habitual reference to the love of Yahweh for his people. The first written form of this tradition belongs to the seventh century, but its definitive form dates from the sixth century (the exile in Babylon); it constitutes the Book of Deuteronomy.

In the Pentateuch, and especially in Genesis (the book with which we are specially concerned here) we find three of these 'traditions' — the Yahwistic, Elohistic and Priestly — placed together and reverently preserved in the biblical text, entailing on occasion a certain duplication

---

[4] *El* is a term to be found in all the Semitic languages to express the idea of God. Thus in Hebrew we find *El*, in Babylonian *Ilou*, in Arabic, *Ilah* (Allah). The root is probably from the verb 'to be strong'. The Hebrew term *Elohim* is in the plural (the Gods, the Divine Powers); this is meant to exalt in some fashion the possessor of the title, just as modern sovereigns use the plural 'we'.

('doublets') and sometimes even different interpretations, at least of detail.

To return to Abram. He cannot have known and uttered the name Yahweh. To allow that he did would be to repeat the anachronism perpetrated by the scribe who belonged to a much later period than the patriarch.

In these circumstances, what was the name given by Abram to his God? Was it Elohim, the God, or rather, the Gods? The term smacks a little too much of polytheism; it was used by all the idolaters to designate the mysterious beings who haunted springs, circles of standing stones or the 'high places' at the tops of mountains.

Could it have been *El Shaddai,* the Rock? This name occurs on five occasions in Genesis. The term, which is used in other books of the Bible, is translated in the Vulgate[5] by the expression 'God Almighty', as it is also in the Septuagint.[6] The Biblical School at Jerusalem (the Dominican École Biblique) has suggested 'God of the Mountain'. In this history of Abram, however, we cannot adopt *El Shaddai* as the term for God; it is far too restricted to this one period.

During the period between Abram and Moses, as a general rule, for the purpose of being recognized by the sons of the patriarch, God named himself as: 'I am the God of Abraham, Isaac and Jacob.' We can conclude, therefore, that at the time of the son of Terah — and even for several generations afterwards — God remained the Unknown, he who speaks and commands, one whose

[5] From the Latin *vulgatum* (in current use). It is the Latin translation of the Bible used by the Church in the West; its text was declared official by the Council of Trent.

[6] The version of the Bible known as the Septuagint is the first translation into Greek of the Hebrew text of the Old Testament. According to tradition this work is supposed to have been carried out about 200 B.C. at the request of Ptolemy II Philadelphus, King of Egypt (284–47) by seventy-two Jewish learned men, hence its name of Septuagint. Nowadays, biblical specialists consider that we have here successive translations, but that their order and chronology is unknown. The work seems to have been concluded towards the end of the second century B.C. It is a very accurate version.

existence and power are acknowledged but whose name is unknown.

Abram leaves the Haran region

Yahweh said to Abram, 'Leave your country, your family and your father's house, for the land I will show you'.

The order was categorical. But before examining the motives for this departure it will be worth while considering exactly what it was that Abram was preparing to leave.

According to the passage quoted he was to leave his country, his family and his father's house. The country was the grassy land of Paddan-aram, the land of the Rivers, where, among all the Aramean tribes dwelling on this pasture land, the patriarch could count a fair number of cousins and relations by marriage. As we shall have occasion to observe in several chapters of the Bible, all these Arameans took care to choose their wives from the pastoral tribes of the same race as their own. Now, for religious reasons, it was important to separate Abram from the idolatrous peoples with whom, by force of circumstances he was regularly in contact. By his 'father's house' the Bible did not mean a building of brick, for Abram and his fellows had always been tent-dwellers. In fact this 'house' was the land of Paddan-aram, the Aramean people, the group of relatives who, on the plain, were to be encountered around the wells or on the bank of a stream to which the animals made their way in the evening. On the other hand, it must not be forgotten that Haran, like Ur at the other end of Mesopotamia, was under the protection of the Moon-god Nannar, the guardian of the city. It was a centre of polytheism in which gods of all kinds swarmed.

In order to form Abram's soul according to his own pattern, to make him his 'priest', to enable him progressively to open his eyes and his heart to divine revelation,

God seems to have decided to segregate Abram and his family on a remote plain, in a semi-desert region where, as God's chosen one, he was to live in relative solitude, no doubt, but in a place suitable for spiritual training.

Blessings and curses

'*I will make you a great nation,*' God promised Abram when ordering him to set off southwards. 'A great nation'? But Abram had no children, for his wife Sarai was sterile. Of course, in accordance with Aramean custom, his nephew Lot was in a position to continue the race and perpetuate his name, but this people could not have been regarded as 'sprung' from Abram, at least in the literal sense of the word.

'*I will bless you, I will make your name so famous that it will be used as a blessing,*' added the Lord.

> *I will bless those who bless you.*
> *I will curse those who slight you.*
> *All the tribes of the earth shall*
> *bless themselves by you* (Gen. 12: 2–3)

Thus Abram received the order to leave the country of Paddan-aram. Once again the patriarch folded his tents, loaded his beasts of burden and departed with his flocks of sheep. The caravan set out towards the land of Canaan, what is now Palestine. God had spoken, his faithful subject obeyed. The history of the Chosen People had begun under the assured protection of the Lord.

3

SHECHEM: THE PROMISE

Abram's arrival in Canaan

So Abram went as Yahweh told him, and Lot went with him . . . Abram took his wife Sarai, his nephew Lot, all the possessions they had amassed and the people they had acquired in Haran. They set off for the land of Canaan, and arrived there (Gen. 12: 4–5). Abram's caravan, following the usual custom, must have gone down along the banks of the Balikh and then back up the course of the Euphrates as far as the large right-angled elbow formed by the river. Here the track finally left the steppe-land; a short journey across the sandy desert brought them without much difficulty to what is now known as Aleppo.

After this, always keeping a safe distance from the cities and cultivated land, the clan set out towards the east of Qatna. Sometimes a halt was made on some pasture land to allow the sheep to rest, sometimes they had to cross, as rapidly as possible, the more or less desert regions separating two oases. It was an exacting journey, exhausting for men and dangerous for beasts.

For geographical reasons it seems likely that the entry to Canaan was effected a little to the north of Lake Chinnereth (nowadays the Lake of Tiberias) where the crossing of the Jordan took place – at this point it is still no more than a brook, easy to ford. The caravan then made a detour to the east, round the edge of the mountainous country in Samaria, and penetrated into the fertile and sheltered valley of Shechem, which is only about 300 feet above sea level; it is surrounded by mountain peaks: to the north, Jebel et-Tôr (the ancient Gerizim, altitude 2900 feet) and Jebel Eslamiyeh (the ancient Ebal, altitude 2950 feet). Shechem was a pastoral centre situated on the watershed between the Mediterranean slopes and the eastern valley of the Jordan, in the heart of the land of Canaan. It was a very wealthy part of the country with rich pasture land crossed by little streams and springs coming from the nearby mountain.

At Shechem, a 'high place' about thirty miles from Jerusalem, the encounter between God and his prophet was to continue and assume a definite form.

Shechem and the Oak of Moreh

Abram passed through the land as far as Shechem's holy place, the Oak of Moreh (Gen. 12: 6).

Shechem and the Oak of Moreh are both terms in need of a certain amount of explanation, for this holy spot and the sacred oak occupy an important place in the history of Israel.

Where exactly was 'Shechem's holy place'? Firstly, of course, it should be noticed that to call it Shechem is to anticipate, for we do not know what this charming valley among the mountains of Samaria was called in Abram's day. The name Shechem only appears long afterwards, at the time, it seems, when Jacob returned from his long stay with his cousin Laban (in about 1750 B.C.). The city was built, it is thought, by Emor the Hivite who gave it the name of his son, Shechem.

For long it was thought that the ancient Shechem

could be identified with what is now the modern Arab village of Nablus. Nablus was Neapolis in ancient times and was rebuilt on the site of the former village by the orders of the Roman emperor Vespasian (A.D. 7–79) who gave it its Roman name. In the Middle Ages the crusaders built a fine gothic church there which has now been turned into a mosque.

Nowadays the historians, archaeologists and geographers of Palestine consider that the site of the camping ground chosen by Abram should not be located at Shechem-Nablus, but rather in a neighbouring district, where there is the tiny village of Balatah, the city of the Oak, in the circumstances an appropriate name. It is a poor village of some twenty houses built on arches and terraces. Around the village stand a few clumps of oaks which local tradition regards as sprung from Abram's ancient oak mentioned in the Bible. A little to the north can be seen the cupolas marking the site of the patriarch Joseph's tomb. On the edge of the village, in a garden, is the famous Jacob's well; here the encounter between Jesus and the Samaritan woman took place.

Regarding the Oak of Moreh it is worth pointing out the results of certain archaeological researches concerning the worship of trees. The excavations undertaken in Canaan have shown that before the arrival of Abram on the territory of what was to become Palestine the Canaanites worshipped the high places, mountains, raised stones, caves, isolated trees and springs. The tree particularly, and it is this which concerns us for the moment, was for the shepherd of the steppes an object of awe and wonder. Even after they had settled in one place the people and farmers of Canaan continued to worship trees, especially the oak, terebinth and tamarisk. The polytheist regarded a tree as the sacred dwelling-place of a living god.

Although before his recent departure from Haran Abram had accepted the worship of Yahweh, we must not harbour illusions on the subject; it took a very long time indeed for Israel to rid itself of certain remnants of its polytheistic practices.

The land of Canaan, the land of the Canaanites

At that time the Canaanites were in the land (Gen. 12: 6).

As the Bible tells us, Abram arrived in the country which we now call Palestine, a country occupied at this period by the Canaanites. Now in a phrase occurring shortly after the quotation given above we learn that God intended in fact to 'give' the land of Canaan to Abram's descendants. It was a project of some magnitude. The Canaanites, with the formidable fortresses which here and there they had built for their defence, would not, it might be guessed, allow themselves to be dispossessed of their land and agricultural wealth by these wandering shepherds with their poor tents and their flocks, often reduced to skin and bone by reason of the droughts. No great pretensions to prophecy were needed to foresee a merciless struggle between these two civilizations of Canaan and Israel. A more dangerous and insidious conflict could also be foreseen at the religious level. Idolatrous customs, Canaanite rites, were accepted by the clan of Yahweh's faithful subjects, thus corrupting the practice of the religion revealed to Abram, spreading their materialist and immoral tenets among the Israelite populace when they came in touch with the Canaanites.

Whence came the Canaanites? They can be regarded as an original branch, like all the Semitic tribes, from the Syro-Arabian steppes (see map, p. 26). Hence, ethnically speaking, if not in every way brothers, they were at least very near cousins of the Arameans, the

group of wandering tribes, scattered over a large part of
the Fertile Crescent, to which Abram's clan belonged. In
about 3000 B.C. a group of these Canaanites settled on
the coast where they set up a sort of maritime and
commercial federation which was known as Phoenicia.
Another party of these same Canaanites seized the
mountain mass and coastal plains forming Palestine
proper. In this connection biblical historians usually
adopt the terminology of the Bible: the name of Canaanites is used only for the Semitic invaders who settled
between the Jordan and the Mediterranean, in the
country which was to serve as the setting for the history
of Israel.

When at the beginning of the third millennium the
Canaanites appeared in this part of the country they
found there a few groups of Neolithics of various races.
In fact, excavation has shown that some of these men of
the stone age, especially at Gezer, cremated their dead,
while at sites not very far away others buried the bodies,
either straight in the ground or in vaults beneath crom-
lechs, menhirs or cairns. Some of these megalithic
monuments still exist in fairly large numbers on the
plateaux in Transjordania and, less numerous, on the
same side of the Jordan. Israelite tradition attributed
these huge constructions to a legendary race of giants
known as *Rephaim*. Prehistorians are not of the opinion
that these pre-Canaanite peoples were Semites. It may
well be that they were Indo-Europeans.

In any case, from 2500 B.C. — that is five centuries
after their arrival in the country — the Canaanites had
practically eliminated these primitive populations (which
in any case were rather thin on the ground) by destruction or assimilation.

The Canaanites swept into the country as a wave of
warlike tent-dwelling nomads, though this formed no

obstacle to their adoption of a settled way of life. Occasionally a tribe, attached to their pastoral traditions, desired to continue living in tents, looking after their flocks. But, generally speaking, the invaders seem to have chosen an urban or agricultural existence. They built strongly fortified cities, fairly far apart with farms raising stock and cereals around them to supply their food. Between these widely spaced cities the countryside was empty and the pasture land as yet belonged to no one. Abram's clan was to find in these great open spaces the opportunity to wander at will according to the needs of the flocks.

It must not be forgotten that the Canaanites were Semites. Far more than their Akkadian cousins, who adopted the Sumerian pantheon and worship, the Canaanites, even after they had settled down, remained attached to their primitive nomadic religion. They kept the gods of their ancestors, Semitic idolatry, the naturalist religion based on the characteristic sexual rites of Arabian religious practice.

As a result, Abram was not long in finding out that the proximity of the Canaanites with their idols constituted a real danger and that the Hebrews, adherents of the new faith, had to be protected against lapsing into the old religion of the desert. This was a constant peril. All these shepherds and slaves of Abram's clan were Semites with an inclination, by reason of their race, to be influenced by the innumerable deities publicly worshipped by the Canaanites. Moreover, for centuries to come the Israelites betrayed a marked attraction for these immoral and orgiastic forms of worship. We can understand that, for these primitive people of the steppes, the lofty and spiritual religion of Yahweh, with no temples, statues or vivid rites, was less attractive than the sensual and spectacular ceremonies performed in the Canaanite

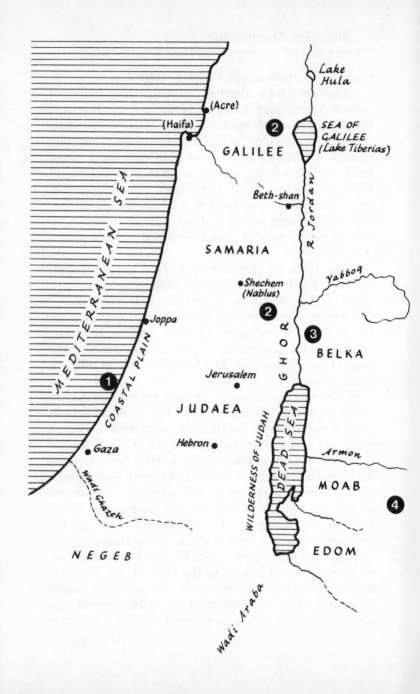

THE LAND OF CANAAN. Ancient Palestine

Smallness of the Land of Canaan

It is quite a small country amounting to a little less than 10,000 square miles (if the territory east of the Jordan is included), smaller therefore than the state of Maryland in the U.S.A. and only a little larger than Wales in the U.K.

The four natural regions of the Land of Canaan

There are four principal natural regions, dividing the country into parallel strips:

1. The coastal plain of the Mediterranean from the Wadi of Gaza (the modern Ghazzeh) to the last spur of the Carmel range.

2. Between the Mediterranean and the Jordan: the hills of the plain of Jezreel (or Esdrelon) continued to the south by the mountain masses of Samaria (or Mount Ephraim) and of Judaea.

3. The Ghor or valley of the Jordan.

4. To the east of the Jordan, between Jordan and the Arabian Desert, the mountain mass of Bajan, Gilead, Moab (in general the mountains and steppes of the modern kingdom of Jordan).

1. The coastal plain

From Mount Carmel to the Wadi of Ghazzeh is the low coastal region, rectilinear in shape (save for the Carmel spur). Along the whole line of coast is a fringe of sand dunes. To the east of these dunes a plain of rich soil brought down by the streams forms the richest region of Palestine. The climate is mild, the soil fertile, and there is enough water. As the east is approached the plain becomes increasingly drier. This is the corn-growing region and is also suitable for cattle rearing. The richness of the soil here forms a strange contrast with the poverty of adjoining Judaea.

2. In the north is Galilee, the land of hills, springs and forests. This pleasant

region is formed by the two mountain masses with the fertile plain of Jezreel (or Esdrelon) in between.

To the south of the plain of Jezreel is the massif of Samaria (with Shechem), undulating country with abundant springs and rich pasture land.

To the south of the massif of Samaria is that of Judaea. The plateau stretches from the Hebron to Jerusalem; there are highlands with a harsh winter climate; it has few springs or streams but wells have been dug almost everywhere. There is little or no forest land and cultivation is difficult, but flocks of sheep or goats can find food on these steppes.

On the west between Judaea and the Mediterranean is the Shephala, the corn-growing district with abundant water.

To the east of the Jordan, the wilderness of Judaea (or Judah) slopes down to the Dead Sea.

To the south of Judaea is the Negeb, a dry, desert region.

3. The Ghor ('hole' or 'hollow')

This is the long rift valley stretching from the Lake of Tiberias to the Dead Sea. Its lowest point occurs where it enters the Dead Sea, 1290 feet below the level of the Mediterranean. The Ghor is a desert through which the Jordan flows; but in the narrow alluvial plain there is plentiful vegetation.

4. The plateaux of the east (Transjordania)

To the east of the Ghor, dominating the rift from a height of 3000 feet, a high plateau rises abruptly and then slopes down to the eastern desert. We can here distinguish the three principal regions mentioned by the Bible:

> To the north the land of Gilead, not unlike Judaea.
> In the centre, Moab, which is fairly fertile.
> In the south Edom, almost a desert.

sanctuaries, located generally on the sacred 'high places', near springs or at the mouth of mysterious caves.

Choice here was wide. There was Baal (the Master), the god of wind, of storm and lightning. Beside him his consort Asherah, goddess of fertility whose naked statue displayed, suitably emphasized, her female characteristics. Elsewhere we find El (the Strong, the Powerful), another celestial being with his consort Ashtoreth (Ashera), often denounced by the biblical writers. Then there was also Adonis (Adonai, the Lord) a young god, of great beauty, the symbol of vegetation. At the end of autumn he was reputed to die, spending the winter hidden in the tomb and rising again in the spring, more attractive than ever. These were the principal Canaanite deities which assumed different names and attributes according to the cities in which they were venerated. Thus Anat and Ashera sometimes appear as kindly protectresses of reborn nature and sometimes as harsh viragos pleased by the horrors of war and living only for bloodshed and massacre. Their emblem was the lion, a bloodthirsty animal.

Around these important personages was a whole host of gods, borrowed from Mesopotamia and Egypt. All was continual movement, with constant transformation or combination. Following the locality a Canaanite deity could adopt another name, or even change sex. There was no lack of picturesque anecdote to explain the changes, the parentage of the gods together with their hates and crimes, and their adulteries and unbridled passions. As if to strengthen the basely material side of this religion the priests adopted human sacrifice and also, as in the Mesopotamian sanctuaries, the official institution of ritual prostitution.

Abram and later on his sons, the patriarchs, had to preserve from this moral contamination the men of their clan and move towards the religious notion of the one, the only, the invisible God whose spiritual demands were far loftier.

The promise made by God to Abram under the Oak of Moreh

Yahweh appeared to Abram and said, 'It is to your descendants that I will give this land' (Gen. 12: 7).

This tree whose Hebrew name can be translated the 'tree of the diviners' owed its name probably to its reputation as a source of oracles. As a rule diviners interpreted the noise of the wind in the branches as the Canaanite deities revealing their will or giving their advice. Thus God was to appear to Abram before this venerable tree to impart to him the unexpected message, 'It is to your descendants that I will give this land.'

'Your descendants.' It was no question here of divine protection granted on occasion to a man or even to a family of shepherds or a small clan of Aramean nomads. The Lord revealed his plan in all its grandeur and simplicity: there was to be a blessing on the patriarch, but also, it can be said, a blessing on his children, on his children's children, on all his descendants in the future.[1] The Chosen People had come into being, even though it was almost by allusion and as yet intangibly. The whole history of Israel, a nation led by God, is already contained in embryo in this utterance of God's in the valley of Shechem. Henceforward God possessed his own group, through which man's moral and religious elevation was

[1] We shall have occasion to observe that for nearly 2000 years it was a question of human descent; later, with Jesus, it was to be transformed into spiritual descent. See, especially, the animated discussion reported by St John. To the Israelites who claimed to be the sons of Abraham Christ answered, 'If you were Abraham's children, you would do what Abraham did' (John 8: 30–59). And in St Matthew's Gospel we read the statement by John the Baptist: 'Do not presume to say to yourselves, "We have Abraham as our father"; for I tell you, God is able from these stones to raise up children to Abraham' (Matt. 3: 9). At Shechem, of course, at the very dawn of biblical history, it could only be a question of family descent.

to be accomplished. The Chosen People is chosen (namely, Abram's descendants) and the Promised Land is promised (that is, the land of Canaan, what we nowadays call Palestine [2]). The history of Israel begins.

Abram followed this further revelation by the Lord with a ceremonial thanksgiving. It was the first sacrifice, it appears, that the patriarch had offered to this God who had led him there. *Abram,* Genesis tells us, *built there an altar for Yahweh who had appeared to him* (12: 7). This was to acknowledge, by a ritual act, the lordship of *El Shaddai* over his clan.

Following certain indications furnished by several later passages in the Bible referring to primitive times, when the nomad tradition was still a living one, it is possible for us to have a clear idea of what the altar 'built' by Abram was like. There was no question, in the circumstances, of faced stone, of cement, of building in the modern sense of the word, since the wandering shepherd, and especially the ancient Hebrews, had an instinctive horror of putting up a solid, permanent building of squared stone or other materials. It is very probable that Abram set up a sort of platform of beaten earth or a kind of offering table of rough stones, merely heaped one

[2] Palestine: in fact, a rather oddly chosen name. Etymologically Palestine means 'the land of the Philistines' (*Pulasati*). The Philistines, probably Cretans, very probably inhabitants of the islands or coasts of the Aegean Sea, were neither Semites nor Indo-Europeans and are difficult to classify ethnologically. They were adventurers who spread into the Syrian lands and even to the Egyptian delta in about 1200 B.C. Ancient writers called these invaders the 'People of the Sea'. Waves of these well-armed, martial warriors seized certain places in Canaan and soon showed their intention of imposing their rule over the wandering tribes. The struggle between the children of Israel and the Philistines appears to us now in a very tragic light. In the face of these fearsome opponents the Chosen People on several occasions were to be within an ace of destruction. The coastal region where the Philistines were established was called Palestine. Unfortunately, this same name, by some sort of geographical aberration, came gradually to be used to designate the interior of the country which had not been conquered by the Philistines. The Greeks adopted this mistaken terminology (Herodotus, 450 B.C.), and the Romans followed their example. Thus ironically enough we find the land of Yahweh's people endowed with the name of its greatest enemy whose domination never really extended over the whole of the land of Canaan.

upon another. There the victim was slaughtered and burnt. Moreover, in a subsequent passage the Bible will shortly give us considerably more detail on the occasion of a curious ceremony in which Abram officiated as a priest.

For the moment it suffices to say that the officiant, the high priest, was by definition the patriarch of the community. There was no priestly hierarchy in the pastoral civilizations. Colleges of priests were only established in history when the people had become established, permanently settled in a particular place with a social organization which had perfected either a system of irrigation or plantations of fruit trees. In the steppes, in the pasture lands or the semi-desert regions the Bedouin sheik is at one and the same time the leader in war, the political head, the principal judge, and by token of this last function, the only one fitted to offer to God a sacrificial victim.

Reference to the liturgy of the ancient nomads, as it is revealed to us on occasion by the Bible, will enable us to reconstruct, in its general outlines, the ceremony at Shechem, which, from the little that we know, must have begun by calling upon God. The people cried out to Yahweh. This was a further anthropomorphic feature, though very excusable in those ancient times: it was advisable to warn the deity, to attract his attention by cries, to make him come to the meeting-place.

And when the deity was there, invisible but present before the table of offerings on which it was intended to offer him the animal, there could be no question of speaking to him in a low voice, but rather in an expressive and intelligible manner. Indeed, it must be admitted, following certain indications in the Bible, that during the sacrificial ceremony those present shouted, even danced, perhaps. This was the way in which it was done among the pagan Arabs. And in biblical history, in like circumstances there occurred strange noisy scenes, with much shouting. On the present occasion the noisy, frenzied acclamations were designated in the Bible by the term *hillel*, a derivative of the verb *yalal*, to yell or roar. In the Hebrew liturgy the moment when the faithful uttered their rather discordant cries was called the *halleluya* (acclaim Yahweh); and it is from this word that Christians have coined the term Alleluia.

At the beginning of the religious meeting those present, joining themselves to the petitions or thanksgiving enunciated by the patriarch Abram, prayed standing, motionless, facing the altar, their arms raised with the palms of their hand facing outwards. That was a posture that was long preserved in the Hebrew ritual. It is Sumerian in origin; the primitive statues from the delta of the Euphrates frequently depict *orantes* in this imploring attitude, a combination of humility, fear and hope.

4

FROM CAMP TO CAMP

Once more they set out on their travels, made but a fleeting halt at Bethel and left again. Frequently they travelled by round-about ways; twice they crossed the Negeb desert, touched on Egyptian territory and came back to Bethel. The time between the first and second halt at Bethel appears to be an interlude. God did not reveal himself again and a fairly long interval elapsed in the dialogue between God and man. It provided for Abram a further period of pastoral life during which we can observe his behaviour as a wandering shepherd.

From Shechem to Bethel

From there [Shechem] *he moved on to the mountainous district east of Bethel, where he pitched his tent, with Bethel to the west and Ai to the east. There he built an altar to Yahweh and invoked the name of Yahweh* (Gen. 12: 8).

They had seemed, after all, comfortably settled at the Oak of Moreh and then suddenly they strike camp and are off. These constant changes of camping ground took place always for the same reason: Abram left the valley of Shechem because there was no longer enough grass for the flocks. And so from the mountain of Samaria they went over to the neighbouring mountain Ephraim, a mere seventy-five miles, or ninety, at the most with the wandering nature of the paths and byways. Mount Ephraim was well known among the wandering shepherds for its rich pastureland, continually freshened by an abundant rainfall.

And so they set out for Mount Ephraim. They camped, the Bible tells us, between Bethel and Ai, that is, on the direct route from Shechem. Here they were some eleven miles, as the crow flies, to the north of a rock on which stood a city of the name of Urusalim, the future Jerusalem. Bethel and Ai, two picturesque names, were also to become famous in biblical history.

Bethel. In Hebrew, Beth'El, the house of God

When Abram, with his men and his beasts, came to this rocky plateau the village of Bethel did not yet exist, nor indeed did the place bear this name; probably it had none at the time. As we shall see, the name Beth'El was given to this site a hundred years later by Jacob, Abram's grandson, after the famous night spent near the small village of Luz. Consequently, Abram a hundred years earlier could not have known the place under the name of Bethel. But the scribe obviously needed a distinctive name to designate, at least approximately, the site of Abram's camp. This place is situated a short distance from the ancient city of Luz (or Luza) which for long remained distinct though quite near the village of Bethel. [1]

Some historians, basing their conclusions on certain ancient ruins which bear witness to a tradition that has endured, are inclined to locate the site of the patriarch's camp on the hill now known as Khirbet el-Bordy, about

[1] Nowadays the ancient Luz and the ancient Bethel form a single village under the name Beitin.

half a mile from the present village of Beitin, the former Bethel. From this hill-top (altitude 2800 feet) there is a fine view: to the east runs the deep valley of the Jordan, enclosed on its left bank by the gloomy rampart formed by the mountains of Moab and Gilead, and even the northern shore of the Dead Sea can be seen; to the west and south the white hills of Judaea can be made out and also certain faces of the rock of Jerusalem.

Ai (or Hai) — the 'ruin' or the 'heap of stones' — was formerly a powerful and ancient city, dating from about the year 3000. But it was destroyed at the beginning of the second millennium; in Abram's time there still remained imposing ruins, hence its name. [2]

There could be only one answer to God's recent revelation, that of thanksgiving. And so once more an altar was put up, this time at Bethel (Gen. 12: 8–9), by Abram, just as he had done at Shechem. The Hebrew shepherd then 'invoked the name of Yahweh', following the rites which were described above in accordance with the evidence which we at present possess. *Then*, the Bible goes on, *he made his way stage by stage to the Negeb*.

The Negeb was the 'dry land', the 'land of the south', 'the southern region'. What exactly was the attraction of this region for which the patriarchs, Abram, Isaac and Jacob, seemed to show a special preference? Certainly it was rather poor country, and some parts of it were rocky and presented a stony and inhospitable appearance. There were rocky, mountainous slopes with little or no rainfall. This unwelcoming, hostile aspect is to be found especially on the slopes going down to the Dead Sea.

[2] When we come to study the various phases of the conquest of the Promised Land under Joshua we shall find the Canaanites making use of this kind of bastion to stem the advance of the Israelites (about 1200). The still imposing remains of Ai were uncovered between 1933 and 1935 on the hill of Ettel, to the east of Bethel.

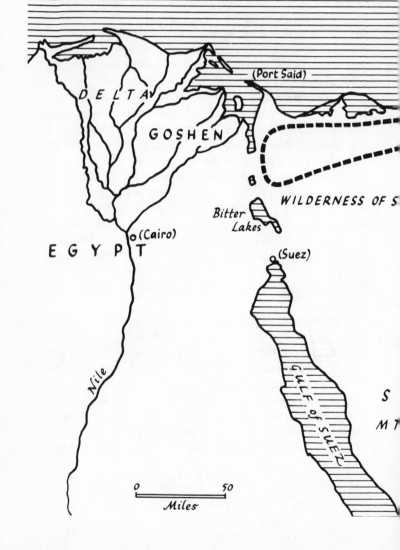

WILDERNESS
OF ZIN

WILDERNESS
OF
PARAN

Abram's round journey: from Bethel back to Bethel by way of the Negeb and Egypt

1. Abram, coming from Shechem in the Ephraim mountain mass, goes on to that of Judaea and sets up his tents between Bethel and Ai.

2. Then, by stages he went forward towards Hebron in the Negeb region (and probably stopped at Beersheba).

3. A famine occurred, as a consequence, probably, of a hot summer which burnt up the pasture, so they went down towards Egypt. In the map an approximative route has been shown, since the Bible gives very little or no precise information about the exact route followed.

4. After a more or less prolonged sojourn, not *in* Egypt but merely in the frontier region of the Delta (the only place where the Egyptians allowed the Bedouins to graze their flocks), Abram returned to the mountain region of Judaea and settled again in the same camping ground that he previously occupied between Ai and Bethel.

On the other hand, on the eastern side the hills of the Shephelah region form a junction with the gently rolling hills of the coastal region. On the eastern side of the mountain mass the land of Negeb contains many valleys, some of them fairly wide; springs are to be found there and water is easily obtainable by digging wells.

In ancient times urban centres appear to have been fairly numerous in this region of the Negeb which can only relatively be described as a desert. Some names recur frequently in the history of the patriarchs: in the first place Beersheba, probably on account of its famous well, and Kedesh, with its pleasant oasis, conveniently placed for caravans on the way to Egypt.

It may well be wondered what secret motive the patriarchs had for their unexpected preference for the Negeb when in the north and the centre of the land of Canaan, on the mountain slopes of Samaria and of Judaea, there was good pasture to be found. It seems that the motive was religious. In the main part of the country there were too many Canaanite cities and too many camps of Canaanite shepherds. Relations with these idolaters obviously provided a constant source of danger for the Hebrew shepherds who would appear to have had an innate tendency to revert to the idols of their Semitic ancestors. They were obliged to isolate their followers or at least to endeavour to lessen opportunities for contact between the two civilizations. Throughout the history of the Chosen People we shall frequently have occasion to observe how the exchange of ideas between the Canaanites, the ancient inhabitants of the country and the sons of Abram, the new arrivals, proved extremely harmful to the development of the high religious standards of the Israelites.

On account of its geographical isolation and the semi-desert nature of the region the Negeb stood out as a quiet part of the country which was almost uninhabited. Here the Jewish religious spirit was to find beneficial solitude and an isolation favourable to meditation on the word of God.

Abram enters Egypt

When famine came to the land Abram went down into Egypt to stay there for the time, since the land was hard pressed by the famine (Gen. 12: 10).

Directly after mention of the Negeb the Bible tells us that Abram decided to 'go down'[3] into Egypt. This can be considered as almost standard pastoral practice, and there is considerable archaeological and historical evidence for it. Obviously there can be no question of thinking that Abram's journey was similar to that of the caravan of Ibsha and his thirty-seven Asiatics which has already been mentioned. Abram's Hebrew clan acted from different motives. At the time when the great droughts dried up the wells of southern Palestine and caused the disappearance of pasture the wandering shepherds used to turn their steps towards the eastern frontier of the delta of the Nile to ask for temporary admission. There at the meeting point of Egypt and the Arabian desert were vast grassy spaces which were endowed with a certain fertility by the seepage of the Nile waters. Pharoah's government made little difficulty about admitting these foreigners who, in the expression current at the time came 'to beg for water'. These unfortunate people did not ask for permission to go 'into Egypt' (as the biblical text somewhat elliptically allows us to think). Indeed, permission for them to enter the

---

[3] Coming from Mesopotamia or Egypt one 'goes up' to Jerusalem. By reason of the geographical relief one 'went down' when, coming from the mountains of Judaea one set out either towards the delta of the Nile or the upper reaches of the Euphrates.

cultivated region was systematically refused; the havoc caused to the farmer by a flock of sheep or goats can easily be imagined. But they were allowed to put up their tents at the extreme boundary of the fields, on the edge of the agricultural region, just as in Mesopotamia the nomads grazed their flocks on the fringe of the steppes. There were certainly no great disadvantages in admitting these shepherds; the Egyptian officials kept a very watchful eye on their movements and, after all, for a time at least, they became tax payers providing funds for the treasury of the Pharaohs.

There is considerable evidence for these removals of the Semites to the eastern boundaries of the delta. At the time of the kings of Heracleopolis (ninth and tenth dynasties, 2300–2160) what is known as the Petersburg papyrus tells us of 'nomads endeavouring to go down into Egypt (obviously the frontier zone is meant) to plead for water, according to their custom and to allow their flocks to drink'. At a later period we read in the Papyrus Anatasi (VI. 4, 15) that in the reign of Merneptah (1224–1210) an Egyptian officer, a frontier guard at Wadi Tumilat (in the Goshen region, to the east of the delta) reports that he had allowed certain tribes of Sasu (Bedouins), natives of Edom (on the Moab plateau), to pass through Pithom and this to enable them and their flocks to live on Egyptian territory. Those are two perfectly typical examples, the first about 350 years before Abram's time, the other some six centuries later than the patriarch's journey as described by Genesis.

This passage in Genesis, which was recorded in writing in the fifth century B.C., at the time when Israel had lost all memory of the daily events of nomad life, undeniably proves for us the remote, indeed the extremely remote origin of the account, and, as a result, its obvious authenticity.

Abram, Sarai and Pharaoh, and the Egyptian adventure

On account of the seriousness of the moral problem which seems to arise on the occasion of Abram's entry into Egypt, it will be better for the Bible to report the facts in its own words.

When famine came to the land [Canaan] Abram went down into Egypt to stay there for the time, since the land was hard pressed by the famine. On the threshold of Egypt he said to his wife Sarai, 'Listen! I know you are a beautiful woman. When the Egyptians see you they will say, "That is his wife", and they will kill me but spare you. Tell them you are my sister, so that they may treat me well because of you and spare my life out of regard for you.' When Abram arrived in Egypt the Egyptians did indeed see that the woman was very beautiful. When Pharaoh's officials saw her they sang her praises to Pharaoh and the woman was taken into Pharaoh's palace. He treated Abram well because of her, and he received flocks, oxen, donkeys, men and women slaves, she-donkeys and camels. But Yahweh inflicted severe plagues on Pharaoh and his household because of Abram's wife Sarai. So Pharaoh summoned Abram and said, 'What is this you have done to me? Why did you not tell me she was your wife? Why did you say, "She is my sister," so that I took her for my wife? Now, here is your wife. Take her and go!' Pharaoh committed him to men who escorted him back to the frontier with his wife and all he possessed (Gen. 12: 10–20).

Philo, Theodoret, Procopius of Gaza, Origen, St John Chrysostom, St Ambrose and St Augustine, and many others besides of the Fathers of the Church have done their best to explain this passage plausibly and to render it acceptable. Nowadays, informed by the history of ancient civilizations in general and of primitive religions in particular, we are in a better position than the theologians of the past to understand the very slow evolution of the human conscience in far off centuries. We are better prepared than our predecessors to grasp the progressive character of the moral ideal down the ages from the remote past to our own days, so that our historical judgement is less likely to be vitiated by anachronism.

Most certainly it is distasteful for us to find this 'righteous man' and 'friend of God' (*El-Khalil*, as even to this day the Arabs call the patriarch Abram), this man chosen by the Lord, agreeing to the revolting action of surrendering his wife for the purpose of ensuring his own safety. It is true, of course, as we have already seen, that Sarai was also his half-sister, the daughter of the same father, not of the same mother. But this explanation could hardly be sufficient to justify Abram's behaviour to the Christians of the first centuries, and still less to our contemporaries. It must be realized, however, that this method of solving Abram's problem was in no way shocking to the men of his times when the moral standard was much lower. In society then the position of a wife, even a legal wife, was not one of any importance. Tribal organization was still founded almost entirely on male supremacy. The female element appeared merely as a superior kind of cattle, destined to provide the offspring necessary for the continuity of the family, but once this function was performed she could expect the minimum of consideration. In addition, the prevalence of polygamy was a constant encouragement to these primitive peoples to regard as of little importance a wife who, after all, could easily be replaced or duplicated. If at this particular moment in time God wished to reveal himself to an individual, a family and then to a nation, to assist the whole of humanity subsequently to rise to a higher state of moral enlightenment, it was precisely because humanity was then at a low moral level.

Indeed we can be sure that Abram's conscience was clear. His contemporaries and the men of his race for some generations to come regarded his behaviour as entirely permissible. Indeed they went further than that. The Hebrew story-tellers and their audiences took particular pleasure in this episode. In the evening before the tent, when the heat of the day had subsided, heads of families would go over the story of Abram and Sarai in the land of the Pharaohs, word for word in the form that they had heard it from the mouths of their fathers and grandfathers. They regarded as a stroke of genius the trick by which the patriarch had outwitted the Egyptian, the worshipper of false gods. Abram had not only avoided the many dangers threatening him but the conclusion of the affair had been even better still – there had been an increase in wealth: *He received flocks, oxen, donkeys, men and women slaves, she-donkeys and camels*.

This way of saving his own life, by giving up his wife and saying that she was not his consort but his sister, was considered so clever that the same anecdote, as related in the Yahwistic version, was to appear only slightly altered in the Elohistic narrative. According to this second version, which is a doublet, Abram was then at Gerar in the southern part of what was afterwards the land of the Philistines, between the Dead Sea and the Mediterranean, a short distance from the coast. There he deceived Abimelech, the king of the country, by passing off Sarai as his sister. But this time Yahweh took care to warn Abimelech in a dream; the latter, fearing for his life, at once returned Sarai to her real husband and, it seemed impossible not to embellish the tale, accompanied the restitution with gifts of 'sheep, cattle, men and women slaves'. It was a clever story indeed, and one that was to figure even a third time in the history of Israel. In this instance it concerned Isaac (Abram's son) and his wife Rebekah. The story was one that never grew stale.

It is not inappropriate to point out that this curious and somewhat embarrassing episode constitutes an excellent proof of the authenticity of the biblical text. For when, after several centuries of oral tradition, carefully preserved in certain religious and secular centres, the various cycles were written down this unseemly adventure was recorded on three occasions: one located it in Egypt, two others place it in Gerar. Now the scribe, who in the fifth century B.C. was entrusted with combining the various traditional texts which were destined to become what we call the Pentateuch, might well have conflated into a single account the three anecdotes which are repeated; or he might merely have ignored them. For at that late period the moral conscience, which had evolved considerably since the time of the patriarchs, could no longer allow Abram's, or Isaac's, behaviour towards their wives to be approved. But in the event the scribe responsible for the text proved himself an honest historian. Not only did he take care not to leave out the 'immoral' chapter, but he was particularly careful to give in full the three versions which have come down to us. No more obvious proof of scriptural authenticity could be desired. Thus we can be certain that the biblical text is here offered to us in its primitive purity, without undergoing manipulation at the hands of a prudish compiler over concerned about public morality.

Abram leaves Egypt, expelled by soldiers

Pharaoh, we glean from the story, was not particularly pleased at the trick played on him by Abram, though we are not told how it was revealed. The Egyptian police of this totalitarian State, as we know from the history of the valley of the Nile, were well organized and given to prying into everything. In any case, reading between the lines, it looks as if the final interview was stormy. *'What is this you have done to me? Why did you not tell me she was your wife? Why did you say, "She is my sister" so that I took her for my wife? Now, here is your wife. Take her and go!'* Pharaoh committed him to men who escorted him back to the frontier with his wife and all he possessed (Gen. 12: 18–20).

Abram left Egypt and, it is hardly astonishing, never returned there. He set out for the Negeb and on arrival at Bethel found there again the altar which he had set up to God. There once more he called on his God to whom, during his sojourn in the idolatrous land of the Pharaohs, he had remained unwaveringly faithful.

Abram, a nomad shepherd

From Egypt Abram returned to the Negeb with his wife and all he possessed, and Lot with him. Abram was a very rich man, with livestock, silver and gold. By stages he went from the Negeb to Bethel, where he had first pitched his tent, between Bethel and Ai, at the place where he had formerly erected the altar. Here Abram invoked the name of Yahweh. Lot, who was travelling with Abram, had flocks and cattle of his own, and tents too. The land was not sufficient to accommodate them both at once, for they had too many possessions to be able to live together. Dispute broke out between the herdsmen of Abram's livestock and those of Lot's. . . . Accordingly Abram said to Lot, 'Let there be no dispute between me and you, nor between my herdsmen and yours, for we are brothers. Is not the whole land open before you? Part company with me; if you take the left, I will go right; if you take the right, I will go left' (Gen. 13: 1–9).

Here for the first time the Bible furnishes us with some details about Abram's pastoral life as a shepherd. It is explained by the fact that he who shortly before was the poor wandering shepherd, whose flocks had certainly been greatly reduced by the terrible drought mentioned above, had now returned from the Nile delta with considerably more livestock. Such details could not be passed over in silence in a pastoral civilization by story-tellers who acted as guardians of the historical tradition. Abram and his nephew Lot (whom he calls his brother) from now on appear in the biblical narrative as important chieftains, rich in flocks and precious metals.

It will be of advantage at this point to consider shortly the customs of these nomads, to observe their daily life and follow their daily existence.

How the patriarch Abram was dressed

Next to his skin the Hebrew of the nomadic period, just like his contemporaries who were settled on the banks of the Euphrates or the Nile, wore a sort of loin cloth. This was the *saq*, a rough and primitive garment, made of wool from sheep, goats or even camels, fastened round the waist by a belt. Memory of the ancient *saq* persisted for long among the people of Israel; from time to time it reappeared on days of mourning or penance.

Thus at the time of Abram the wandering shepherd wore a garment covering him from the waist to the upper thigh. There was nothing in the nature of a shirt. The *sadin*, which came into use at a much later period, was always reserved to the wealthy and, more especially, to elegant women.

Over the loincloth, the Hebrew of Abram's time had a choice of two garments. Either, for the poorest or for those who had heavy physical labour to perform, a sort of skirt fastened at the waist and reaching a little lower than the knees, the upper part of the body remaining unclothed, or else a tunic, made of a large square of cloth falling from the neck to the calves. Usually this tunic was fastened over the left shoulder, it then went down crosswise over the chest and under the right arm, to which it left freedom of movement. It was a woollen garment often woven of many colours and adorned with embroidery. For boys and girls this tunic was fairly long, coming down almost to the ankles.

The mantle was the outer garment. At first it was a single piece of cloth, though in Abram's time it would already have been provided with holes for the head and arms. In any case, it was the forerunner of the modern Arab's burnous. It was absolutely indispensable for protection against the low temperatures at night in the open air or in a tent. Thus, even at periods nearer our own the law forbade a creditor to keep a mantle, received as a pledge, after sunset; the lender was obliged to return, at least for the night, this garment which, serving both as a cloak and a blanket, was wrapped round the body for sleeping. At the early period with which we are concerned the cloak must often have been made of the skin of an animal, since speaking of Esau (the third generation after Abram) Genesis informs us that he *was red . . . as though he were completely wrapped in a hairy cloak* (Gen. 25: 25).

Women's clothes differed from men's by being of an appreciably ampler cut with a gaudier colour scheme. Generally, a woman covered her head with a veil but the law imposed no obligation to lower it. Frequently in the Bible women appear with their faces uncovered, even before strangers.

Shoes had soles of wood, reed or palm bark. An arrangement of straps attached them to the feet, as we can learn from more than one allusion (see Gen. 14: 23).

Abram and all his family were provided with clothes as protection against the sun in summer, the rain of winter and the cold nights. They were shod for long journeys on foot across the pebbly stretches and the burning sands of the Negeb, or when they had to go from one oasis to another over the desert trails.

Abram's tent

The nomad was very proud, and regarded it as a matter of tremendous importance, that he lived in his own tent, the symbol of his complete freedom and independence.

In the early stages of the history of the nomadic tribes of shepherds animal skins were sewn together to make a waterproof tent. But already by Abram's time women were spinning and weaving long bands, as wide as the looms then in use would allow, and so produced a rough but very resistant cloth, a very dark brown in colour. Hence the expression used by the Bride in the Song of

Nomad tent

Songs, *'I am black but lovely . . . daughters of Jerusalem, like the tents of Kedar'* (1: 5).

We have no precise information about the patriarchs' tents since the Bible gives no details on the subject. In fact they can scarcely have differed from those still used nowadays by the Bedouin. The covering is held up by a certain number of poles between about four and a half and six feet high. The dimensions of the tent obviously vary according to the importance and the wealth of the occupant. Normally, there are two distinct parts separated by a thick curtain forming a partition. The front section is that belonging to the men; ordinarily this part is wide open over its whole width. Behind it, the section reserved for the women and children is kept firmly closed, hidden from the prying gaze of outsiders. Sometimes in the largest tents this section is divided up by an arrangement of curtains so as to form several cells, for the slaves and the servants, for the kitchen and lavatory.

These tents are put up by the nomads with extraordinary skill and speed, yet the physical effort required is a heavy one. The operation is performed as follows: the covering is first laid out flat on the ground and one or two men with poles then slipped underneath. The heads of these poles, which fit into a specially backed socket in the cover, are then raised and the poles pushed into the ground. It now only remains to fix the tent firmly to the ground: long guy ropes are inserted into wooden hooks attached all along the edge of the tent and firmly fastened to pegs previously driven hard into the ground. Taking down the tent is an even more rapid operation.

The furniture in Abram's tent

There were no chairs or tables, and people sat cross-legged on woollen carpets, reed mats or tanned skins. For eating they all squatted on a circular leather mat round a large dish into which all dipped with their fingers. One piece of kitchen equipment that should be mentioned was the flour mill. In ancient times it was composed of two parts, a slab of very hard stone (basalt as a rule) slightly concave in form, and a flat, medium sized stone which was pushed backwards and forwards with both hands to grind the grain. It required a considerable physical effort and was very hard work; as a result it was left to the women.

In the tent, hanging from the poles, especially in the room at the back, the women's quarters, were skin containers holding water, of course, but also wine, milk and oil. These curious skin bottles retained the shape of the animal, goat or even pig, whose skin had been used; the tail and feet were cut off and these ends were sewn up and made waterproof by a coat of pitch. The spout was constituted by the neck (the head had been removed); instead of a cork the neck was bound up tightly with twine.

The lamps at this period were very simple. They were in the form of a small clay cup, circular or oval with a lip made by pinching together a part of the rim. It was only later that this shape, just beginning to emerge in the ancient examples, gradually developed into a spout. Flax, hemp or a hollow rush were used for a wick.

Abram's flocks

In the first place we must be clear about the class of nomad to which the patriarchs belonged. It would be an anachronism to liken them to the nomads of the great Arabian desert who appear to have been camel breeders; these were tireless caravaneers and, usually, resolute brigands. This was a truculent, almost epic form of nomadism, on the grand scale and entirely amoral. It had nothing in common with the quiet, peaceful, almost bourgeois form of nomadism adopted by Abram the shepherd and his descendants.

In ethnological terms these wandering Bedouin, like Abram, are known as breeders of smaller livestock. With their sheep and goats they camped either on the grassy steppes on the edge of the cultivated land (as we saw occurred in Sumeria) or on the natural pasture as yet belonging to no one (as we have just observed in Canaan, their new dwelling-place). Once the grass in one place had been grazed they left for other pasture land, which had, of course, to possess a well or a spring where men and beasts could quench their thirst. Before long the shepherds had established a kind of regular circuit, always going from the same oasis to the same piece of pasture, from the water source to the same valleys. They came thus to have established routes over the length of which they considered, in accordance with the unwritten law of the nomads, that they possessed grazing rights.

'Breeders of smaller livestock': this expression seems automatically to exclude the ruminants, cows and oxen, which would be unable to bear the long journeys under semi-desert conditions — three days without drinking, which means nothing to sheep or goats. And yet the Bible mentions the calves and bulls which Abram offered to the Lord. How is this to be explained?

It has just been pointed out that Abram's clan, which had grown to some importance on leaving Egypt, had arranged the routes for its flocks, so that they were regularly moved at fixed dates to different places with periodical returns to watering-places. Near each of these wells they took care to set up guard posts to prevent brigands from destroying their equipment, and on occasion these sentries were entrusted with the care of a few cows and calves. Thus the cattle could graze the scanty grass of the neighbourhood near the drinking-place, and with the help of a small store of hay laid up during the good season they managed to eke out an existence. This is the explanation of the allusions in the Bible to the calves and bulls belonging to a group of nomads. It meant that there was a fixed establishment, though of a rudimentary kind, separate from the clan which, always on the move, could, after all, obtain on occasion a few head of cattle.

The existence of the small farm also enabled the occupants to sow and harvest some cereals although, generally speaking, pasture land and corn land are different in character, but this primitive arrangement should not be regarded as showing any tendency to a settled agricultural way of life, in the proper sense of the term. Life was still organized on a nomadic and pastoral basis; the planting of fruit trees alone constitutes the sign of man's definitive settlement on the land.

Your servants are shepherds, like our fathers before us (Gen. 47: 3). They were shepherds, raising and looking after smaller livestock, by which was meant sheep and goats.

Abram's sheep and those of the Hebrews at the time of the patriarchs were probably *Oves laticaudatae* (wide-tailed sheep) a kind which can still be seen in Palestine. Certain passages of Genesis and Leviticus inform us of the characteristics of this caudal appendix which contained a large proportion of fat. More precise information still on the subject of this animal of the land of Canaan is furnished by the historian Herodotus and the naturalist Aristotle: the tail, which was extremely fatty, was made up of adipose tissue capable of providing the body with water during those periods when the beast could not be taken to a drinking-place. It is a huge and rather inelegant organ which may weigh anything up to about twenty pounds.

These sheep's tails provide the Bedouin with a dish of which they are very fond; it is cut in slices and fried. Sheep or ram's tail, down the ages, was often brought to the altar of Yahweh to be offered as a sacrificial gift. The fat from these tails was also used in cooking and provided the oil for lamps.

Abram's sheep were rarely completely black though few again were entirely white. Rather were they pied, that is, a mixture of black and white; on the fully grown animals the coat assumed a faded appearance which, with the advance of age, became increasingly general.

It is difficult to obtain an exact idea of the numbers in Abram's flocks. The Bible gives us to understand that when he left Egypt he owned a considerable number, but no figure is mentioned. Nowadays, the westerner who visits the Near East is often astonished at the huge flocks to be encountered in Transjordania. Does that mean that Abram, the owner of much livestock was a great meat-eater? Not at all. The sheep was raised, principally at least, for the production of wool. Its coat was used, in the first place, to provide the raw material for the clothes of the shepherds and their families. The women were spinning and weaving all the time. The same material was used to make tents. In addition, wool was the basis of the trade established between the nomad and the citizens of the land of Canaan. Thus bales of wool were bartered for sacks of corn, manufactured articles, and also bars of gold and silver which were carefully stored under the tents. Sheep, as the producers of wealth, were hardly ever used for meat. Obviously in certain circumstances one was offered in sacrifice to Yahweh, but for these gifts to the Lord the shepherd usually preferred to take a ram or a lamb (a male, of course). It is only in La Fontaine's fables that a countryman kills the hen which lays the golden eggs.

In fact the patriarchs' diet was basically one of milk (of sheep or goat) and cereals (bought from the farmers of the country). It required some special event which interrupted the daily routine, the arrival of a guest, for example, even an unknown one, for the chief to give the order to kill one or several head of livestock.

The flock was there not to provide meat but wool. Thus among these tribes of shepherds in charge of many thousands of sheep, the great popular celebration was always, and everywhere, the sheep-shearing.

Can we mention wethers in this context? The Law expressly forbade the offering on the altar of any animal which had undergone castration. *You are not to do that in your country* says Leviticus (22: 24). Was it merely the offering of a castrated animal which was thus forbidden? Or was it the fact of mutilation? Josephus, the Jewish historian, enables us to say that it was the second, for he tells us that castration of animals was strictly prohibited in Israel (*Antiquities of the Jews,* IV, 8, 40). Probably this prohibition with regard to domestic animals was suggested by the horror with which the Israelites regarded human castration. Thus there can be no question of wethers in speaking of the flocks of the shepherds of Israel.

In addition to sheep there were the goats. On the long marches for change of pasture as well as on the pasture land itself and at the drinking places, both kinds of animals were herded together, without disadvantage. According to the characteristic details furnished by the Bible the goats of the Hebrew nomads were probably of the kind known as *Capra membrica,* easily recognizable by its well-developed horns, by its height and chiefly by its drooping ears. It was black in colour, as was mentioned above, and the poet without forcing the image excessively, could speak of the hair of the beloved, hanging down her neck, as *like a flock of goats frisking down the slopes of Gilead* (S. of S. 4: 1).

The coat of these Canaanite goats was made up of two sorts of hair. On top was a rather rough long fleece which was used especially for tent cloth. Beneath there was finer hair which, although short, was soft and woolly. The spinners valued the goat particularly, and also the cooks, for goats' milk was especially good and even in the time of the patriarchs cheese was made. Goat kid, too, furnished a tasty dish on occasion.

It is difficult to speak with equal certainty about the camel, and it is not even certain whether the camel had yet been domesticated.

When he left Egypt and the Nile delta Abram had become, we know, a wealthy shepherd, the owner of many flocks and of fine ingots of precious metals. Among his animals the Bible mentions the camel. Archaeologists have objected that this animal is not represented on the monuments of the Pharaohs until a much later period. But the camel might have already been employed in the usual way on the semi-desert fringes of the Nile delta; and Abram's camp was confined precisely to this frontier region. There seems, therefore, no reason why it should not be granted that the Hebrew clan, which had lately grown wealthy, might have possessed a certain number of dromedaries (camels with one hump).

At the time of Isaac's marriage, when it was a question of providing him with a bride, Abram, who at that time had established his camp in southern Palestine, sent his slave, Eliezer, with some camels, to Haran on the Upper Euphrates, the 'land of his kinsfolk'. This long journey, nearly a thousand miles there and back, required camels if it was to be done in reasonable time, but mention of camels may have been an anachronism.

The shepherds must have led a dreadful life. To provide

At the end of the day — the drinking trough

the flocks with enough grass the different pastures had
to be at some distance from each other. The man in
charge of the flocks was obliged to live in isolation. He
had always to be on the alert, on the look-out for an
animal which wandered away, a ewe dropping a lamb,
a lamb that was sick. The shepherd was responsible for
his sheep; he had to defend them against thieves and also
against wild beasts, of which there were many, always
on the watch for prey. There were wolves, much feared
at that period, and lions which found refuge in the
impenetrable woods bordering the Jordan.

The dogs used were a mongrel breed of jackal, about
the size of a wolf-hound, very fierce and hardly domesticated, trained to attack wild beasts. These dogs did not

fear to try conclusions even with a lion. Their function was one of protection rather than of watching that the flock did not stray.

Every evening the shepherd led his flock from the pasture to the drinking place, usually made up of wooden troughs or clay cisterns arranged near the well. The curb, as we have seen, was nothing like those to be found in the European countryside. It was very wide, anything from about four and a half to nine feet in diameter. It was practically at ground level with a low wall to prevent the animals falling into the water. The well at Beersheba, dug by Abram, which since those remote times has hardly been modified in its general form, shows how the walls have been worn by the cords used in pulling up the skins or vessels. When camp was struck the well was covered over by wide slabs of stone, and over these a thin layer of earth was spread in order to render the spot invisible to the Bedouin brigands who were always bent on destruction out of sheer malice. If the opening of the well was smaller than usual it was always covered during the day by a heavy stone which, in the evening, was moved away on the arrival of the flocks.

The flocks came to the well in closely packed ranks. The shepherds kept them at a distance, as the animals went to the troughs in turn and on the order of their own shepherd; the different flocks could not be allowed to mix without causing disputes and quarrels. It was each shepherd's task, of course, to draw the water and fill up the troughs for his own flock. This was very hard work indeed. Life as a shepherd was really very arduous and exhausting.

Food in the time of Abram

Although it is not possible to establish with certainty the

order in which dishes were served at a meal in Abram's time, we can at least enumerate the basic foods, what was eaten and what drunk in the tents of Abram's clan.

There was very little meat in the daily diet, except of course on a religious festival or when a guest of some distinction was entertained. Then, depending on the importance of the visitor, a goat or a lamb, a sheep or an ox was slaughtered. If it was a very special occasion indeed, with a certain ostentation a fatted calf was prepared.

Sometimes hunting made an important contribution. The Deuteronomic law allowed as food the stag (no longer to be found in Palestine), the gazelle (its name of *cibeya*, the graceful, was often given to the Israelites' daughters), fallow-deer (but it is not entirely certain what was meant by the term, for this animal appears never to have been common in Palestine) and roe-deer (some archaeologists are inclined to the view that a variety of antelope was intended).

These meats were accompanied by various vegetables: onions, cooked or raw, leeks, lentils, chick-peas and beans. Everything was well seasoned with garlic. Then there were the celebrated 'bitter herbs'. These were merely salads (chicory, lettuce, endive) with which were mixed cress, parsley or sea holly.

Among the birds the Bible often mentions the dove, the poetical name for pigeon. Several varieties of birds were found in Palestine. A great favourite was the quail, a migratory bird which in the autumn came from Europe on its way to Africa. The return journey was made in the spring. Sometimes they made a landfall and then could be easily taken by hand. The nomadic tribes also caught the red-legged partridge (also known as the rock partridge) which were plentiful in the mountainous region of Judaea and also the yellow partridge (known as the sand-partridge) whose habitat was on the banks of the Jordan.

Fishing was practised principally in the north of the country, in the Jordan and its tributaries, in Lake Huleh and, especially, in the Sea of Galilee. There could be no question of the shepherds confined to the south of the country obtaining freshwater fish and only with difficulty could they get sea fish. But both kinds, when dried, were the object of intensive trade throughout the country.

Another food, much appreciated by the nomads, was neither flesh nor fish. This was the grasshopper. Almost as if to compensate for the famines caused by these insects in their destruction of the crops grasshoppers were sometimes eaten by the shepherds. They were gathered by the basketful at sunrise when they were still sluggish with the cold of the night and their wings were heavy with the dew of the dawn. Abram must certainly have enjoyed a good dish of grasshoppers. They were boiled or roasted (the head and wings being first removed) and sometimes they were dried in the sun. The women used also to reduce them to powder and thus obtained a small supply of flour which was made palatable by seasoning with salt or honey.

Sugar was unknown at this period; honey was used in its place. For these wandering shepherds it could only of course be wild honey, extracted from the rocks of the Judaean desert where it had been stored by the bees. It was used for making cakes and was mixed with milk and butter, and its medicinal qualities were appreciated.

But the basic food was milk with its normal derivatives. The Hebrew shepherd, who was the owner of innumerable goats and sheep, drank milk throughout the day. Often the nomad was better able to provide a bowl of milk than a jar of water. Genesis mentions the various kinds of milk that were used; they were that of ewes, camels[4], cows and asses. The milk was kept in leather bottles where the heat soon turned it sour; the nomads found it a refreshing drink and regarded it as a delicacy. To make it into butter it was placed in a skin hung from the branch of a tree or between three stakes arranged in a triangle; by using sticks to shake it a product was obtained, known in Hebrew by the name of *hem'ah*, translated as butter, but it could just as well be cream or curds.

Together with milk, bread formed the essential food of the patriarchs and their men. Thus in all the meals mentioned in Genesis bread is given the place of honour. This essential food was produced in rather a crude fashion. Very early in the morning the women ground the corn. The rough flour thus obtained was mixed with water and salted; the dough was then placed on stones which had previously been heated in a shallow ditch. These loaves, round and of medium size, could also be baked over charcoal, but in that case they had to be turned frequently with a stick to prevent their burning.

The loaf thus produced was of the same consistency throughout with neither crust nor crumb. Eaten hot it was tasty enough, stale it was rather dull. Then in the semi-desert regions, it should be remembered, there were scarcely any trees; as a consequence the only fuel obtainable was that made by the dried droppings of the animals; this often gave the bread a disagreeable taste.

Leaven was added to the dough but only when there was time to make the bread in this way, or if a part of the batch was to be kept until the next day, but generally unleavened bread was eaten. Usually barley flour was used, wheat flour being kept for special occasions.

The Old Testament also provides some information

[4] It seems that at the time of Abram the camel was not yet regarded as an unclean animal. Later it was so classified, and then camel's milk was forbidden to the Hebrews as a drink.

about cakes; it tells us in detail the kind of paste used, the shape and the different ways of cooking them. The housewife was well aware of the great importance of the raw materials; wheat flour was greatly preferred. Unleavened girdle-cakes were kneaded with honey or oil and, like the bread, they were cooked over heated stones in a brazier, or beneath hot cinders. They must have been something like a hardened and brittle pancake.

Cucumbers, water melons, melons — the people of Israel were always fond, and still are nowadays, of these cucurbitaceous fruits. Figs and pomegranates, apples and grapes, olives, purchased or stolen from the settled farmers, were also eaten. There were no oranges as these were only introduced into Palestine after the Mohammedan conquest (seventh century A.D.). There is no mention of dates, either in the Old or New Testament (except perhaps in 2 Sam. 6: 19 and 1 Chron. 16: 3) although the palm tree was very common throughout the Near East.

Wine occupies a place of honour in the Bible. Scripture scholars have estimated that it is mentioned no less than 141 times. It is sung by the Psalmist, praised in the Book of Judges, extolled by Zechariah. But there is an anachronism to be avoided; wine is the drink of the city dweller, of the peasant settled on his own land. In the shepherds' tents water or milk was drunk.

Before concluding this investigation into the subject of Abram's food it will be necessary to examine the delicate question of 'clean' and 'unclean' animals as it is laid down in Leviticus. This law was enacted, it must be recalled, well after Abram's time so it may well contain prohibitions unknown to the patriarch. Nevertheless, Leviticus gives us an idea of a whole body of ancient ritual regulations (Lev. 3, for example) and it is very probable that Abram knew the principal articles.

The following is a summary list of the foods forbidden to be placed on the altar and, for the same reason, on the domestic table: the hare, pig, dog, cat and later the camel. Of the creatures living in the water only those could be eaten which had fins and scales, that is, fish in the ordinary sense. The proscribed birds were principally the carnivorous ones, eagles, crows, etc. All reptiles were also forbidden and all insects with the exception of certain grasshoppers and locusts.

Nowadays, ethnologists think that these forbidden foods, among the Hebrews as indeed among the peoples of all latitudes, are to be explained by the idea of a taboo. This is a practical means of self-protection against spiritual dangers. Primitive peoples (those of the pre-historic period as well as those of the present day) believe that certain animals possess a divine or demoniacal power. They think that by eating a piece of meat the spiritual qualities of the flesh that is consumed are assimilated. Therefore certain animals are regarded as dangerous for eating by men of the tribe. It is a simple matter of prudence.

We come now to the method of cooking and the way in which the meals took place in the tents of the shepherds.

There was a formal prescription that no animal could be eaten unless the blood was first drawn off. For the blood was the 'soul' of the animal, which amounted to saying that it was 'the life of the flesh'. Now life belongs to God and that is why the blood of the animal was to be poured out on the earth or offered to God. Directly the animal had been killed (generally by a man) it was skinned and taken to the women entrusted with its preparation.

When it was to be roasted the whole carcase was fixed on a very large spit over a wood fire. If it was to be boiled the slaughterer cut up the carcase, beginning operations with the right shoulder; then he took the pieces to the cooks.

It is not surprising that the kitchen utensils used in the tents were simple and few in number. Hanging from pegs were the skins containing water, milk, oil and melted butter. On the ground were a few earthenware vessels of a rough pattern. Earthenware jars were used also by the women who carried them on the shoulder, a graceful gesture of great distinction, when they fetched water from the spring. There was also a small set of wicker-work baskets for bread and fruit. But the nomad, who did not take kindly to the refinements of daily life, left to the comfort-loving city dwellers of Canaan and the wealthy farmers the use of metal utensils (copper, tin, bronze). The shepherds kept to their earthenware vessels.

To store certain liquids hollowed-out horns (from bulls or rams) were used, just like our modern bottles. Meat was cut with a copper or bronze knife. A long heavy fork of the same metal was used to take the pieces of meat from the pots.

Boiled meat and vegetables were cooked in water with a seasoning of salt (generally from the Dead Sea) or even spices. For choice dishes meat was cooked in milk, also in oil or even in liquid butter. In normal times, that is, outside the periods of famine due to drought, the food was swimming in a plentiful and fatty gravy.

Before the meal all the members of the family washed their hands. Afterwards they squatted on a large leather carpet stretched on the ground, gathering round the dishes which were brought in. On a large dish were meat and vegetables. In a kind of pan was the gravy. Each guest was given his piece of bread. With a certain ceremony the head of the family handed round the portions. There were no spoons, forks or knives; fingers were used. The bread served as a plate (for the meat), and as a spoon for the gravy into which each one dipped as he liked.

Separation of Abram and Lot

After his long circuitous journey and his adventures in Egypt Abram returned and camped again at Bethel. There, the Bible tells us, *Abram invoked the name of Yahweh* (Gen. 13: 4). That is a very significant observation.

'Abram invoked the name of Yahweh.' This means that during his journey to the land of the Pharaohs Abram remained constant to his belief in God, and was not corrupted by the dreadful polytheism of Egypt with its deified beasts and monsters. These gods of the valley of the Nile must have been observed by Abram at the doors of the sanctuaries or in the avenues of the sphinx; he would have seen their colossal carved effigies at the entrances of the temples or the fortresses which were to be found even in the frontier zone of the delta.

Thus, immediately on his return to Bethel, it was fitting to show clearly that he had remained unwavering in his fidelity to his God. On arrival at his old camping-ground 'Abram invoked the name of Yahweh', in other words the envoy wished to show that he had in no wise failed in his mission; he had carefully kept the message entrusted to him; there had been no compromise with polytheism.

On the other hand, Abram seems to have emerged from the expedition very successfully. His flocks had multiplied and his 'tents' (that is, his shepherds, servants and slaves) showed an extraordinary increase in numbers. It was the same with Lot, his nephew who, from what the Bible says, seems to have possessed his own flocks and establishment. As was to be expected, the usual difficulties soon occurred. The pasture was insufficient to feed so great a number of stock and in addition there were clashes between the shepherds at the wells. In the evening, when they had to take their turn at the drinking places, they quarrelled. It was time to separate. That indeed was the ordinary process. Once a clan had grown too numerous it divided in two. In this way were constituted the tribes, federations of clans derived in principle at least from a common origin.

Abram, lording it over his nephew, allowed him to choose his pasture. From the natural viewpoint provided by Bethel there was an immense sweep of country to be seen. In the distance was the valley of the Jordan and nearer the shores of the Dead Sea with the plains bordering it on the southern side. As a background stood the lowering mountainous country of Moab. Lot had only to say where he would go. *'Let there be no dispute between me and you,'* said Abram, *'nor between my herdsmen and yours, for we are brothers. . . . Part company with me: if you take the left, I will go right; if you take the right, I will go left'* (Gen. 13: 8–9). The conciliatory spirit could be pushed no further.

Lot needed no pressing, and since his uncle had allowed him to choose he took good care that his choice should be a good one. He chose the pastures in the valley of Siddim, to the south of the Dead Sea, in the neighbourhood of the cities of Sodom and Gomorrah.

It was no doubt necessary for Lot to disappear, not indeed from the history of the Hebrews but at least from Abram's clan. In this way Abram remained the head of the family, alone before God. He was available for service. In this land of Bethel, which for several religious reasons the people of Israel regarded as an especially sacred place, the time had come when, for the third time, Yahweh was to manifest himself to Abram.

At Shechem God had revealed his general plan which,

105

though expressed in lofty terms, was still not very explicit: *'It is to your descendants that I will give this land.'* A gift of this nature, it is clear, required confirmation in more solemn form, and at Bethel God gave further information. As we have seen, and it is a point of some importance for the understanding of what happened, from his camp Abram could look down on an immense panorama of the valleys, pasture land and plains of the south. God explained to the patriarch that all this constituted the future domain of his children.

Yahweh said to Abram: *Look all round from where you are towards the north and the south, towards the east and the west. All the land within sight I will give to you and your descendants for ever. I will make your descendants like the dust on the ground: when men succeed in counting the specks of dust on the ground, then they will be able to count your descendants!* (Gen. 13: 14–16).

But the agreement had not yet been sealed, so to say, in solemn form. It was at Hebron that this occurred in the great ceremony of the eternal Covenant granted by God to his people. To this end God gave a command: *'Come, travel through the length and breadth of the land, for I mean to give it to you.' So Abram went with his tents to settle at the Oak of Mamre, at Hebron* (Gen. 13: 17–18).

5

MAMRE: THE COVENANT

Ur formed the starting point of the small Hebrew clan, the 'people from beyond the river', on their great and mysterious adventure; Haran was the pastoral setting for God's revelation; Shechem, at the Oak of Moreh, was the place of the Promise; Bethel was the place where the promise was confirmed and made explicit. And now at Mamre, quite close to Hebron, once again under an oak, the ceremony of the Covenant was to take place.

At the Oak of Mamre

Abram went with his tents to settle at the Oak of Mamre, at Hebron (Gen. 13: 18).

Bethel, situated to the north of what was to become Jerusalem was far too near to the important trading routes and to those Canaanite cities where idolatrous and obscene forms of worship were well established. The nomad shepherds definitely preferred the highlands of Judaea where the scarcity of the population ensured almost complete isolation.

Thus there was another journey and another camp. They settled some twenty miles to the south of the rock where already was established the Canaanite city which was one day to become the holy city of Jerusalem. This time the camp site seems to have been well chosen since

Abram settled there for a very long time and it was there that he was to die.

The Oak of Mamre, like the Oak of Moreh, was certainly one of the numerous sacred trees such as were held in reverence by the idolaters as the dwelling-place of a deity. These trees were sometimes reputed to furnish oracles. The Oak of Mamre stood nearly a mile north of the village of Hebron at the place now known as Ramet el-Khalîl, 'the hill of the Friend'

Abram's counter-attack

News was brought to Abram that four Mesopotamian kings, whose names and titles are given by the Bible[1], had invaded the southern part of the country. When they arrived before Sodom and Gomorrah the 'kings' of these two cities gave battle but were routed. After their victory, won in the country bordering the Dead Sea, the Mesopotamians set off home taking with them, in accordance with the custom of the times, prisoners and booty. The survivor who brought the news to Abram told him also that Lot and his clan, who had settled at Sodom, formed part of the horde of prisoners now on their way to the Euphrates.

Without delay Abram armed three hundred and eighteen of his men ('members of his household from birth') and with 'his allies' went in pursuit of the raiders. Somewhere near Dan, right in the north of Canaan, near the source of the Jordan, he fell upon the rear-guard of the invaders, taking them by surprise; in their triumph they had not allowed sufficiently for a counter-attack. Abram succeeded in setting Lot free and returned south with him

[1] Amraphel, king of Shinar; Arioch, king of Ellasar; Chedorlaomer, king of Elam; and Tidal, king of the Goiim. Modern historians have so far been unable to identify any of these names in the royal lists of Mesopotamia, but they belong to Mesopotamian or Elamitic nomenclature of this ancient period. These 'kings of Mesopotamia' give the impression of being petty kings (*patesi*) or even merely Bedouin chieftains.

together with *all the goods . . . and his possessions, together with the women and people'*. In other words with the whole clan.

Biblical commentators agree that this chapter does not belong to the Yahwistic or Elohistic sources; it is rather a warlike account which finds a natural place in the history of nomads.

The mysterious meeting of Abram and Melchizedek

Melchizedek, king of Salem brought bread and wine; he was a priest of God Most High. He pronounced this blessing:

'Blessed be Abram by God Most High, creator of heaven and earth,
and blessed be God Most High for handing over your enemies to you.'

And Abram gave him a tithe of everything (Gen. 14: 18–20).

This is a very mysterious part of the story. Abram was on his way back from the north of Palestine after the defeat of the four kings of Mesopotamia and the liberation of Lot. To regain his camp at Hebron he took *the Valley of Shaveh, that is, the Valley of the King*. Josephus says that this place lay within a quarter of a mile of Jerusalem. Suddenly, with nothing to prepare us for the encounter, there appears an astonishing personnage – Melchizedek, king of Jerusalem. According to the exegetes these verses of Genesis were inserted after the composition of this chapter, which belongs to a special category and is very ancient. The literal sense of the verses is this.

Melchizedek, king of Salem (very probably Jerusalem) comes to congratulate Abram on his recent victory. By Abram's military operation Melchizedek was freed from certain danger. On the other hand, he was well aware that Abram represented a by no means negligible force and thus his gesture was intended as a token of friendship towards the victorious patriarch. He therefore brought with him choice provisions, bread and wine, for the men exhausted by the fighting during the previous days. Abram, not wishing to be outdone by the king, gave him a part of the booty obtained in the battle. Mutual blessings were pronounced to the 'God Most High' (*El-Elyon*); this name was attributed by Melchizedek to his God (Shalem, regarded as the great god of the region). Abram, who knew the only true God, had no intention of starting a theological discussion; he accepted the blessings of Melchizedek, but attributed them to Yahweh. After this meal Melchizedek disappears from the historical annals of the Hebrews as suddenly as he had appeared. That is all, in the literal meaning of the passage.

But we have here the first contact of Israel (in the person of its father Abram) with Jerusalem. And this explains why the sacred writer recorded this ancient memory with such care.

This is the first time that we encounter the symbolism of the episode which recurs on different occasions in the Old and New Testaments. In addition, David, after capturing Jerusalem, for that reason was to become the representative, that is, the priest, of the true God who was acknowledged as the only 'Most High', a priest of the order of Melchizedek, because he was king of Jerusalem. Subsequently, Melchizedek was regarded by theologians as a figure of the Messiah; they did so following the text of Genesis and the Psalms, whose origins go back to a thousand years before our era. At all events, after this warlike interlude Abram returned to his camp in the oak-grove at Mamre.

The three encounters with God at the Oak of Mamre

On the 'high place' of Mamre God revealed himself on three different occasions. On each he delivered a message which had a considerable effect on the history of the sons of Israel.

First encounter: the Covenant between God and his people; a son is to be born to Abram, the gift of the land of Canaan to the descendants of the Hebrew chieftain.

Second encounter: confirmation of the perpetual Covenant; the institution of circumcision; announcement of the birth of a son to Abram and Sarai, who is to be called Isaac.

Third encounter: three mysterious persons arrive at Abram's camp; Yahweh is the head of this little group; confirmation of the birth of Isaac which is to be in a year's time; Abram pleads that the destruction hovering over Sodom and the accursed cities be turned away.

There were therefore three divine manifestations, interspersed with certain social events whose importance should not be neglected.

First encounter with God under the Oak of Mamre: the Covenant (Gen. 15)

According to the Bible Abram had a 'vision', during which he had a conversation with God. Two points were established: the promise of a son and the repeated promise of the land of Canaan. In conclusion there took place a strange archaic sacrifice intended to seal the Covenant.

Faced with these very general, not to say vague statements by God, for the first time Abram shows evidence not of disbelief but at least of a certain reasonable worry. After all, God keeps on speaking of Abram's descendants, but Sarai his wife is barren. He had no child to succeed him, and one of his slaves, probably Eliezer, would

111

inherit. How in these circumstances could Abram count on a 'reward', taking into account the social importance attached in the east to succession in the direct line?

God replied with a correction: the patriarch's heir would not be the slave in question, but a son of his own flesh and blood. The innumerable stars in the night sky provided an apt comparison: *'Look up to heaven and count the stars if you can. Such will be your descendants.'* At once Abram put his faith in Yahweh's promise. At the human level the realization of this promise appeared impossible, but Abram's was real faith.

Yahweh had just predicted to the aged patriarch the birth of a son, and now he was going to bestow on him, as his personal property, for his descendants, the land of Canaan. But how could Abram imagine that this country, dotted with formidable strongholds defended by garrisons should be his; how could he believe that his clan would seize all these prosperous farms and cities defended by a highly organized military aristocracy? It seemed beyond comprehension.

Abram's very understandable reaction is hardly surprising. Promises were hardly enough, now a little proof would be welcome. God was about to give it to him in the ritual ceremony of the Covenant. This Covenant, granted by God of his own accord, unilaterally, could only be solemnly promulgated during an impressive sacrifice.

The traditional requirements for such a sacrifice were well known: *'Get me a three-year-old heifer, a three-year-old goat, a three-year-old ram, a turtledove and a young pigeon.'* Abram obtained all these, cut them in half, and put half on one side and half facing it on another with a sort of path between with room to walk. This was an ancient Sumero-Akkadian rite; the contracting parties went forward together between the divided carcases, each accepting in advance the fate of these victims if they ever violated the promises made to the other.

And now Abram fell into a deep sleep. Yahweh appeared to him and told him that his descendants would go to a foreign land (the future migration of the clan of Jacob to Egypt) and that there they would undergo oppression for the space of four centuries; in the fourth generation they would return to the land of Canaan.

The sun had just set and night came down. To seal the agreement in the Mesopotamian manner Yahweh made ready to go between the halves of the victims, as was explained above. But on this occasion it was Yahweh alone who carried out the gesture because the pact was unilateral. God could not treat man as an equal. He 'gave' of his free will and pleasure, without the creature having any rights in the matter. It was he who settled it and laid down what was to be done. He bound himself, but only in relation to himself.

How did God show himself? In his deep sleep Abram saw *a smoking furnace and firebrand* that went between the halves. In this way Yahweh made his Covenant in the following terms: *To your descendants I give this land, from the wadi of Egypt to the great river, the river Euphrates*[2] (Gen. 15: 18). After which life continued with its daily work and concerns, but we may well imagine the direction taken by Abram's thoughts.

Quarrel among wives

Between the deep experience just described, together with the ceremony of the Covenant and the second

[2] The southern frontier of what was to become Palestine was very accurately stated: the wadi of Egypt (wadi El-Ghazzeh to the south of Gaza). But on the subject of the northern boundary it looks as if the scribe's stylus has wandered a little, for the frontiers of the Promised Land never reached the Euphrates; more unpretentiously they stopped in the neighbourhood where the Jordan rises.

encounter with God, which was soon to be followed by a third, all at the Oak of Mamre, there took place an incident provoked by the behaviour of the two women of Abram's family, the wife (Sarai) and the concubine (Hagar).

Sarai was hopelessly barren. And throughout the Near East it was a shameful thing for a woman to be unable to provide for the continuance of the line. Fortunately, Sumerian law provided her with a legal means of obtaining a child; she was allowed to choose from among her slaves a serving girl whom she could bestow on her husband as a concubine. If the servant conceived she gave birth 'on the lap of the wife' and according to Mesopotamian law the new-born child would be regarded henceforward not as the concubine's son but as the lawful wife's. In short, it was a shrewd method of adoption in which the father's rights were safeguarded.

As it happened there was soon dissension in Abram's family circle. Hagar, the Egyptian slave given to Abram by Sarai as his concubine, became pregnant. At once she began to behave very disagreeably towards her mistress, though it is possible that Sarai was not the soul of patience. In short, there was soon open war between the two women. Sarai informed Abram of the whole affair, complaining bitterly of being treated with scorn by a mere slave girl. According to Sumerian law the lawful wife could treat the concubine as she liked so long as the latter had not given birth. So, asked for his advice Abram replied, *'Treat her as you think fit.'* This was not cowardice on Abram's part; his behaviour was entirely in accordance with the prescriptions of the Sumerian code. Accordingly Sarai 'treated her so badly that she ran away from her'.

Hagar set out in the direction of Egypt, her native land, but to reach the banks of the Nile she had to cross the desert of Negeb and the wilderness of Paran, a foolish undertaking on her own for it meant almost certain death. At a spring on the road to Shur, some distance from the frontier, God appeared to her. A moving and dramatic dialogue now took place.

'Hagar, slave-girl of Sarai, where have you come from, and where are you going?' God asked.

'I am running away from my mistress Sarai,' she replied.

'Go back to your mistress and submit to her,' said God.

There followed a series of promises concerning Hagar's descendants; her son Ishmael was to be the ancestor of the Arab race. *'I will make your descendants too numerous to be counted.'* Then Yahweh uttered this prophetic verse in which can be felt all the wildness of the desert Arab:

Now you have conceived, and you will bear a son,
and you shall name him Ishmael,
for Yahweh has heard your cries of distress.
A wild-ass [3] *of a man he will be, against*
every man, and every man against him, [4] *setting*
himself to defy all his brothers. [5] (Gen. 16: 11–12).

Hagar now gave to Yahweh and the well of Shur names whose meaning is difficult to grasp. According to the Jerusalem Bible the text of Hagar's words is certainly corrupt, and the site of the well (near Bered, an uniden-tified place) appears very uncertain.

[3] Wild ass: probably the species *Equus onager* (*E. hemippus*) of Central Asia. In its morphological characteristics it is half donkey, half horse.

[4] Like the wild ass, which is unmanageable and almost impossible to tame, Ishmael, the son of Abram and Hagar, the Egyptian slave, was to grow up to be warlike, half-wild or at least very unsociable. His descendants, the desert Arabs, breeders of camels, were to follow his example.

[5] *Setting himself to defy all his brothers.* Here we have noted the psychological opposition complex of the wandering Arab who is bitter, and the avowed opponent of everything that is not to his taste.

115

Hagar thereupon returned to the camp. History is silent on the welcome that she received from her mistress Sarai. The child which was subsequently born, following the divine command was called Ishmael. For the time being peace was restored in the patriarch's tent, but Sarai bore a grudge and trouble seemed bound to recur.

Second encounter with God at the Oak of Mamre

The Covenant had been proclaimed at Hebron beneath the Oak of Mamre. Soon afterwards it was confirmed under the same sacred tree. What is the reason for these repetitions? Should they be regarded as textual doublets, belonging to different cycles, one to the Priestly, the other to the Yahwistic? Not necessarily.

It should not be forgotten that God was dealing with a Bedouin, only lately an idolater, a polytheist, and only of average moral stature. It could hardly be expected that on the strength of one command received in a mysterious manner this shepherd should suddenly entirely transform his religious convictions which were deeply rooted in him by a Semitic atavism already some thousands of years old. Although at the first summons Abram responded with faith, it remains true, nonetheless, that these successive confirmations need not be regarded as useless repetitions.

The four points laid down by God at the second encounter at the Oak of Mamre (Gen. 17)

First point

Yahweh recalls the terms of the contract which he had drawn up of his own accord.

From Abram will come forth peoples and also kings.

To Abram's descendants will be given the land in which he is living at the time, that is, the land of Canaan. They will own it in perpetuity.

116

Second point

God changes the names of Abram and his wife. *'You shall no longer be called Abram; your name shall be Abraham. . . . As for Sarai your wife, you shall not call her Sarai, but Sarah.'* Hebrew scholars who have examined the linguistic problem are quite clear on the point: Abram and Abraham mean the same thing, 'He is great by reason of his father', that is, 'He is of noble descent'. The same applies to Sarai: both Sarai and Sarah are linguistic variants meaning the same thing, namely, 'princess'. In these circumstances what was the reason for this twofold change of name which, in actual fact, is not a change at all?

It should be said in the first place that in the Near East, and especially in ancient times, a person's name is not, as it is in the West, a mere social label intended to distinguish among themselves the members of a family. A name possessed a power of its own, bestowing on the individual who received it special moral and physical qualities. That is why at a turning-point in his life a man could be led to adopt another name, whether he chose it himself or it was imposed on him by a supernatural power. It was a change which marked and indicated his new destiny, and can be compared with the change of name by a priest or a layman on entering certain religious orders, or the adoption of a new Christian name by the Pope when he is elected.

Thus for the Semite the name expresses something of the inner nature. As a result knowledge of the name of an individual meant knowing his underlying nature and being able to exercise a certain hold over him. Therefore to give a name was, in the first place, to reveal the knowledge one possessed of the nature of a man, an animal or even a thing (for example, Adam gave the animals their names); then, too, it meant also taking possession of this being or thing in some way and exercising over it a certain authority.

The change of name effected in this case by Yahweh means therefore that God knew Abram and Sarai (which is obvious), but also that he took possession of them, that henceforward the couple belonged to him in a very special way; that was the effect of the Covenant.

Third point: circumcision

Now this is my Covenant which you are to maintain between myself and you, and your descendants after you: all your males must be circumcised. You shall circumcise your foreskin, and this shall be the sign of the Covenant between myself and you. . . . My Covenant shall be marked on your bodies as a Covenant in perpetuity (Gen. 17: 10–11, 13).

Circumcision is a very complicated question. To be understood it must be seen in the context of the Near East in ancient times. Very probably it originated among the central races of Africa; it seems to have been adopted quite early by the Nubian tribes of the Upper Nile, and subsequently by the Egyptians at a very distant period. Proof is provided by some paintings in the hypogea dating from the earlier dynasties (2400 B.C.) and also by the mummies of the same period. For long historians believed that in Egypt circumcision was confined to soldiers, priests and men of learning. This is untrue and it is known nowadays that the practice extended to all social classes.

The African rite had thus penetrated to the country of the Nile, then it spread to certain parts of the Near East. Although it was unknown among the Babylonians and Assyrians, it was practiced among most of the neighbours of Israel (Canaanites, Phoenicians, Edomites, Ammonites and Midianites). The Egyptian custom was adopted by a great proportion of the Semites and through them it spread to many countries in the Levant.

The practice of circumcision is to be found among many peoples of the Near East professing different religions, a proof that the rite had no theological significance. It seems to have belonged rather to the sphere of sexual magic; it was an initiatory act of social character.

So circumcision was of African origin, was very old, was to be found almost everywhere throughout the Near East and was derived from tribal rather than religious concerns. In these circumstances it seems difficult to explain why Yahweh should have chosen as the sign of the Covenant with his people this 'mark' of such little originality and one adopted already for centuries past, even thousands of years, by so many idolatrous religions of the region.

By the Covenant established by Yahweh under the Oak of Mamre circumcision was soon destined to become, in the religious history of Israel, the symbol of spiritual and moral initiation. Ritual mutilation should not be compared with the external mark made upon a sheep or a goat. Hebrew circumcision is rather a sign, marked on the body, and intended as a constant reminder to man that there is in him something to be given up, to be cast aside: that is, his evil inclinations, the impurity of his thoughts, the corruption of his spirit. Moses was the first to teach the deeper significance of circumcision. *Circumcise your heart then and be obstinate no longer* (Deut. 10: 16). Further on he made this comment: *Yahweh your God will circumcise your heart and the heart of your descendants, until you love Yahweh your God with all your heart and soul* (Deut. 30: 6). Spiritual circumcision meant rejection of all that proved an obstacle to the love of God and observance of the Law.

119

Ritual mutilation was certainly faithfully observed at the time of the patriarchs. There are numerous examples to show that it was practised at the nomadic pastoral period, but after that, when the Hebrews were settled in Egypt at first as voluntary immigrants and subsequently as slaves, and subjected to forced labour in large-scale building operations, it appears that gradually they forgot this custom and that it fell into abeyance. Moses himself was uncircumcised and so remained. But when the Chosen People, finally freed from the yoke of the Pharaohs, were able to return to Canaan, Joshua, Moses' successor, and the leader of the Hebrews, required the circumcision of all males, whatever their age, directly they entered the Promised Land. From that time the ritual custom, a real reminder in the body of Yahweh's faithful follower of the ceremony of the Covenant, was practised continuously among the Hebrews and then among the orthodox Jews.

Fourth point

God announced to Abraham the impending birth of a son who would be his heir. Without accepting the figures given by the scribe for the ages of Abraham and Sarah it must be admitted that both he and his wife were already advanced in age. Hence Abraham's very human reaction to Yahweh's unexpected statement: *I will bless her,* he said, *and moreover, give you a son by her. I will bless her and nations shall come out of her; kings of peoples shall descend from her* (Gen. 17: 16). Abraham considered the material impossibility of such an event taking place; he bowed to the ground to show his deference, but he could not help laughing to himself; for he was too old, much too old to hope for a son, and Sarah, too, had long passed the age of child-bearing.

Abraham imagined that God was alluding to Ishmael,

the son of the Egyptian servant Hagar, the patriarch's heir who, by the Babylonian legal fiction, could be regarded as Sarah's own son. And yet Yahweh had spoken in the future tense: 'I will give you a son!' Abraham, in oriental fashion, endeavoured to obtain clarification and somewhat cunningly answered Yahweh, *'Oh! let Ishmael live in your presence!'* But it appeared that it was nothing to do with Ishmael. He had been blessed. He was to beget twelve sons and be the father of a great nation. (We may remember that the Arabs regard him as the ancestor of their race.) He can be left to his destiny.

And now Yahweh stated, clearly this time, that he meant indeed a son according to the flesh for Abraham and Sarah. His name was to be Isaac (meaning 'May God Smile'), an allusion to Abraham's laughter which expressed both his disbelief at hearing this humanly unrealizable promise and his joy at the idea of such great and unexpected happiness. Yahweh went on: *'With him I will establish my Covenant, a Covenant in perpetuity.'*

Finally, therefore, under the Oak of Mamre, in the very place where the Covenant had been drawn up between Yahweh and his faithful follower, four points were now clearly established: the confirmation of the Covenant; the change in the names of the patriarch and his wife; the introduction of circumcision among the Hebrew clan; the promise of the birth of Isaac.

God's third visit to the Oak of Mamre (Gen. 18)

Abraham, the Bible tells us, was sitting by the entrance to his tent during the hottest part of the day. Suddenly on looking up he saw three men coming towards the camp, three strangers, for Abraham had not yet recognized who they were. The head of the group was Yahweh in person. His authority and power were to shine out, as we shall see, from the least of the words he uttered. But so far he had said nothing, and for the moment walked straight to the patriarch's tent, followed by two servants — two 'angels' as we are told in the next chapter — that is spirits serving God. At the sight of these strangers coming towards him Abraham got up quickly and, still unaware of with whom he had to deal, ran to meet them, for the law of the steppes imposed exacting duties towards isolated travellers who passed by the nomad's camp.

According to the centuries' old custom prevailing among the shepherds the traveller who thus passed by the boundary of the camp had a right to hospitality in the tent of the chief himself. In any case a stranger who passed in sight of the tents was always invited to halt for a while. He would be received with eagerness combined with a certain ostentation. In the first place, of course, the Bedouin chieftain was always pleased to receive admiration for the richness of his flocks, the sumptuous-ness of his furniture, the number of his slaves. In addition, the stranger often came from afar and was the bearer of political news, and might be in a position to recount interesting personal experiences. In the evening after a meal he would be asked to tell stories of his life and the outstanding historical events of his tribe. Hospitality does not merely impose duties, it often provides uncommon pleasure.

Thus Abraham got up and, so the Bible tells us, *ran* to meet the three men. It was right and proper to show eagerness towards someone who was shortly to be one's guest, even if he were completely unknown. In eastern fashion, with the exact emphasis suitable to the circum-stance, the patriarch bowed to the ground before the three men. And to the leader, whose identity he had not yet guessed, he addressed this request, in the poetic and exaggerated manner dear to the Semites: *'My Lord . . .*

I beg you, if I find favour with you, kindly do not pass your servant by. A little water shall be brought; you shall wash your feet and lie down under the tree. Let me fetch a little bread and you shall refresh yourselves before going further. That is why you have come in your servant's direction.' It was flowery language no doubt, but the language of the times, and to regard it as obsequious would be to fall into a clear anachronism. It was important in the first place to wash the feet of a traveller worn out by a long journey. And directly after this obligatory ceremony came the announcement of the meal, care being taken, of course, to offer a very simple one out of humility (though it is true that *lehem* means both bread and food). 'Do as you say,' replied the unknown man to whom these remarks had been addressed.

At once an impromptu meal, though a sumptuous one, was got ready. The patriarch urged Sarah on. *'Hurry,'* he said, *'knead three bushels of flour'* (obviously it was a real banquet), and not barley or ordinary wheat flour but the finest quality wheat flour. *'Knead,'* ordered the patriarch, *'and make loaves'*. Next, he ran to the cattle, chose a fine and tender calf, brought it back to the tent and told the servant to kill and prepare it.

Abraham reserved to himself the honour of serving the strangers whom he had made comfortable close to the tent in the shade of the oak tree. He set the meat before them in person, together with milk and curds. And while the three men, seated on the ground, dipped their hands into the dish, Abraham ceremoniously remained standing near them. The three travellers ate in silence. Suddenly their leader questioned Abraham: *'Where is your wife Sarah?'* It was a surprising question from one who was not a member of the clan; he was obviously very well informed about the patriarch's family. *'She is in the tent,'*

123

replied Abraham, for the women were kept at the back of the tent, partitioned by a goatskin curtain. Nevertheless, by means of cunningly arranged slits they did not miss much of what went on among the men, especially when there were guests.

Once more the guest spoke to Abraham: *'I shall visit you again next year without fail, and your wife will then have a son,'* he remarked. From her hiding-place Sarah followed this strange conversation with avid curiosity. She thought to herself: *'Now that I am past the age of child-bearing, and my husband is an old man, is pleasure to come my way again?'* And she laughed to herself.

The leader of the three (Yahweh, as we know, and Abraham had by now guessed who his guest was) had his back to the tent, but he had no need to see with his eyes to discover what was going on behind him. Continuing to speak to Abraham, he asked: *'Why did Sarah laugh and say, "Am I really going to have a child now that I am old?"'* Hearing these words, Sarah who was still behind the partition was afraid. This man who had never seen her and yet knew her name, who was aware that she was there listening to the conversation so tactlessly, who read her thoughts and had heard her silent laugh, who could he be but some supernatural being? Her fear can be understood. She tried to get out of it by lying, and intervening in the conversation, uttered a forthright denial: *'I did not laugh,'* she said. *'Oh yes, you did laugh,'* replied Yahweh.

Previously Abraham had laughed during his second encounter with God at the Oak of Mamre when the birth of Isaac was foretold. Now it was Sarah's turn to show her disbelief or at least her surprise by laughing. As we know, God had already said that the child was to be called Isaac, that is, 'May God smile, may God be kind.'

Some little time previously Abraham had recognized

Yahweh in the form which he had assumed in the circumstances. With his characteristic faith the patriarch now received the confirmation of the prophecy: *'At the same time next year I shall visit you again and Sarah will have a son.'*

The biblical account of the destruction of Sodom and Gomorrah

At the end of the meal the three guests accompanied by Abraham set out towards Sodom and Gomorrah, two cities, at no great distance away in the valley of Siddim, which by their dissolute morals were regarded as the symbol of depravity. As they went along the account depicts Yahweh conversing with Abraham as with a friend (*El-Khalil*) and telling him that he intended to destroy these cities and the Canaanite territory where such abominations took place. With marked deference, but also with a certain persistence, Abraham interceded for them, asking for mercy; he tried to show God that by systematically destroying these places he might punish the righteous dwelling in them, and emphasized that men who had not shared in the sin did not deserve to be put to death. In characteristic eastern fashion they now began to haggle over the conditions under which mercy could be shown; in this can be clearly seen the emerging notion of love of neighbour and there is revealed also the efficacious role of the saints in protecting the world. The reader must refer to this passage in the Bible; it is too long to be reproduced in full here and too fine to be summarized (Gen. 18: 16–33).

Yahweh then went away and Abraham returned to his camp at Hebron; meanwhile the two 'angels' of Yahweh continued on their way and entered Sodom where Lot, Abraham's nephew, had settled after the division of their flocks. The angels received hospitality for the young Hebrew chieftain. During the night frenzied men of the

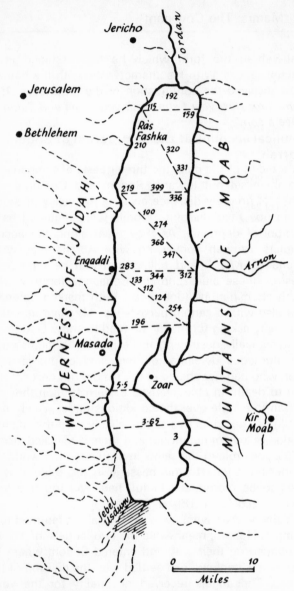

Note. Dotted lines indicate the *wadis* which flow only intermittently at the rainy season. Figures indicate the depth of the water in metres.

THE DEAD SEA

Some figures

Dimensions of the Dead Sea: north to south, 53 miles long, widest point, 10 miles; area 340 square miles.

The level of the Dead Sea, according to the seasonal variation, is between 1290 and 1293 feet below the Mediterranean.

The deepest points reach a depth of 1311 feet.

On the diagram opposite it will be observed that to the south of the Lisan peninsula the depth is almost insignificant; 18 feet at the narrowest point, 10 to 12 feet in that sort of southern pool in which the Bible locates the catastrophe of Sodom and Gormorrah.
(see explanatory maps on pp. 130 and 131)

The Dead Sea is one of the water areas richest in salt in the whole world: a proportion of 242·6 per 1000. The density of the water varies according to depth between 1·160 to 1·230. No fish or living thing can exist in this saturated salt solution.

Nearly seven million tons of water per day from the Jordan and a further seven million from other streams flow into the Dead Sea, but the very high rate of evaporation compensates for this.

The various names of the Dead Sea

The Bible usually calls it *yam hammelah,* salt sea or sea of salt. Sometimes, too, sea of solitude or sea of the plain. In contrast to the Mediterranean it is also called oriental sea.

In the Talmuds we find the names, Sea of Salt, or Sea of Sodom.

Josephus, the Jewish historian (about A.D. 37–100), calls it Asphalt Lake (on account of the asphalt contained in it) and also Lake of Sodom.

It was the Greeks, followed in this by the Latins, who called it the Dead Sea.

In the thirteenth century of our era the Arab geographer Idresi called it the Sea (or Lake) of Za'ra (Zoar); he adds that it also bears the name of Lake of Sadum (Sodom) and of Ghamura (Gomorrah).

For Islamic Arabs the Dead Sea is known under the name of the Sea of Lot as in the Koran Mohammed recounted the dramatic story of Abraham's nephew, miraculously saved from the seismic catastrophe.

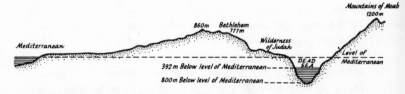

Section of the Mediterranean as far as the mountains of Moab, passing through the Dead Sea.

town surrounded Lot's house demanding loudly that the two new arrivals should be surrendered to them: *Where are the men who came to you tonight? Send them out to us so that we may abuse them* (Gen. 19: 5). Lot tried to reason with them but the situation began to look ugly. Miraculously, the attackers were struck blind, thus enabling the besieged to leave the house at once. Whereupon the angels warned Lot of the imminent punishment hanging over the city. *'We are about to destroy this place,'* they explained to Lot, *'for there is a great outcry against them, and it has reached Yahweh. And Yahweh has sent us to destroy them'* (Gen. 19: 13). This was because there had not been found the ten righteous men who would have enabled Abraham to obtain a general pardon for the place. When dawn broke the angels insisted once more on Lot leaving the city quickly: *'Come, take your wife and these two daughters of yours, or you will be overwhelmed in the punishment of the town. And as he hesitated the men took him by the hand, and his wife and two daughters, because of the pity Yahweh felt for him. They led him out and left him outside the town.'* Lot was instructed to run for his life. *'Neither look behind you nor stop anywhere on the plain. Make for the hills if you would not be overwhelmed.'* But the hills were some way off; Lot therefore requested that he should be allowed to go to a small city nearer at hand. This was granted, and although the city had been condemned it was spared for Lot's sake, since he had taken refuge there.

The sun had scarcely risen when *Yahweh rained on Sodom and Gomorrah brimstone and fire. . . . He overthrew these towns and the whole plain, with all the inhabitants of the towns, and everything that grew there.* At that moment Lot was entering Zoar; he was safe from the catastrophe.

One of the angels had urged on Lot and his family not to tarry in their flight and not to look behind them. Lot's wife in the scramble did not obey the order; at one moment she stopped and could not prevent herself glancing back over the burning city. At once she was turned into a pillar of salt.

The whole story, full of dramatic detail, must have enchanted the Hebrew audience when a practised story-teller, faithful to an unchangeable oral tradition, narrated the vicissitudes of this 'moral' tale, with the destruction of the wicked cities, the disappearance beneath a rain of fire of the whole of this accursed valley of Siddim close to the southern section of the Dead Sea.

What the geologists can tell us

Soundings taken in the Dead Sea have revealed the extraordinary shape of this basin. According to work carried out by geographers of the Near East the bottom of the Dead Sea appears to be divided into two clearly defined parts (as can be seen on the diagram on p. 131, the Dead Sea after 1850 B.C.). Beside a very large chasm about forty-eight miles long and running to a depth of 1311 feet, to the south, a much smaller and far shallower basin may be observed. Now this part lying only some fifty to sixty-five feet below the waters corresponds exactly to the region mentioned in the Bible, the valley of Siddim and the region of the accursed cities of Sodom and Gomorrah.

In addition, in this southern part of the Dead Sea, known to ancient times as the Salt Sea, an observer in a boat a short distance from the shore when the sun's rays are at a certain angle can perceive submerged forests covered with a thick deposit of salt, which has ensured the preservation of the trunks and main branches of the

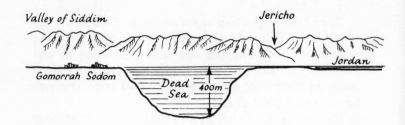

Explanatory maps of the subsidence of the Plain of Siddim, presumed sites of Sodom and Gomorrah.

At this date the waters of the Dead Sea had not yet invaded the Plain of Siddim where stood Sodom, Gomorrah, Admah and Zeboiim, the cities accursed for their wickedness.

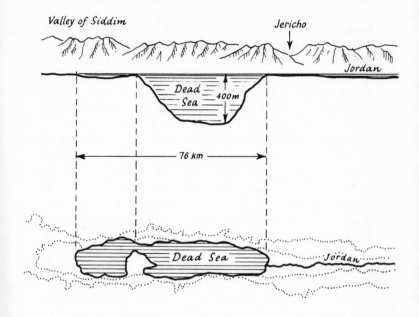

The Dead Sea after the catastrophe of 1850 B.C. (section and plan).

At this date the subsidence of the valley of Siddim was brought about by an earthquake. Although the bottom of the Dead Sea is about 1300 feet below the surface, the depth of the later part, over the former plain of Siddim varies between about ten and eighteen feet.

trees. These skeletons of vegetable life appear to date from a remote period. Thus it seems that in this place a real subsidence occurred and the vegetation crystallized in salt under the water, so preserving the evidence of a former forested and probably agricultural region. There was no certainty of this, of course, but at least a strong presumption that it had happened in this way.

The necessary scientific proof was finally furnished, it seems, by the American geologist Jack Finegan who in 1951 drew up a very interesting report at the conclusion of his investigations conducted on the spot: 'It appears that it was in about 1900 B.C. that there occurred the great cataclysm which destroyed Sodom and Gomorrah. A study of all the literary, geological and archaeological evidence leads to the conclusion that the cities of the plain (Gen. 19: 25) were located in a region at present covered by the waters which gradually invaded the southern part of the Dead Sea, and that their destruction resulted from a serious earthquake, probably combined with an explosion, lightning and the escape of natural gas and widespread fire. (See pp. 130–131, the diagrams of the Dead Sea before 1900 B.C. and after 1900 B.C.) It is quite usual, indeed, for a subsidence, whether gradual or sudden, to produce faults allowing the escape of magmatic substances.

It should be added that this series of subsidences continued afterwards. The city of Zoar, in which Lot took refuge after his hurried departure from Sodom, suffered a further and very serious earthquake at the time of the Roman occupation; subsequently a part of the city was battered to pieces by the waves of the Dead Sea. This small urban centre, rebuilt a short time afterwards on the hillside, was inhabited until the Middle Ages.

Quite a short visit to the site would convince the most decided sceptic that an earthquake could have taken place. The underground fire in the vicinity, the hot springs, the sulphurous vapour given off by certain hollows, the bituminous wells, mentioned in the Bible, the crystals of salt covering the rocks, the blocks of salt scattered over the countryside, all show clearly the volcanic nature of this region. And finally there is the presence of this inland sea, called the Asphalt Lake with its viscous, sticky, salt-laden water in which the human body cannot sink and where no fish, shell fish or water plant is to be found. It is the Dead Sea in a dead land, and a visible token of the ever latent geological accident. The biblical version of the disappearance of the valley of Siddim beneath the waters of the Dead Sea accompanied by the destruction of the cities (showing clearly the effects of an earthquake shock) can therefore be accepted as historically possible, since it is so clearly authenticated by the geographical data of the site.

In the anecdote of Lot's wife transformed into a pillar of salt for her disobedient curiosity we may perhaps perceive the memory of some tragic accident which has been embroidered upon in the popular imagination. To the west of the southern portion of the Dead Sea, over a distance of some twenty-five miles, runs a small chain of mountains almost exclusively made up of crystals of salt, gleaming in the sunlight like diamonds. A great number of the salt blocks have been hewn and carved by the rain and have assumed odd forms; from a distance some of them could be taken for human shapes.

Abraham's knowledge of the earthly paradise, the flood, the tower of Babel, etc.

Nowadays it is admitted that in the sixth or fifth century B.C. compilers putting the different chapters of the Bible in order placed a sort of summary of the prehistory of the people of Israel at the beginning of the work, as a preface,

immediately before the history of Abraham. It seemed
logical and obvious to place some sort of narrative of the
creation of the world and of man before the account of
the patriarch's life.

These ideas (creation, earthly paradise, flood, tower of
Babel etc.) now form part of our spiritual, artistic and
literary heritage; in what form could Abraham have
known them? Was his so clear a view as that which we
possess today? The reader might be tempted to think so
since the events in question come immediately before
the story of Abraham. But the Bible is a book which
must be interpreted with every possible precaution.

The difficulties in connection with the literary history
of the first eleven chapters of Genesis are well known.
Without going into details of this somewhat complex
study, which would require lengthy explanations, we can
investigate what the patriarch can have known of the
origins of the world and the creation of man.

The text of the Bible dealing with the creation is a
Yahwistic account, dating from the tenth century B.C.
The writer of the first pages of Genesis has used within
the general plan of his narrative certain Sumero-Akkadian
traditions, some elements of which were known to
Abraham as well as to the many generations who came
after him. Indeed it is not so much in the account given
by the Bible as in several cuneiform texts that we are
able to discern the belief of Abraham about the creation
of the universe and the first man.

There is nothing surprising about this. It is worth
pointing out here, indeed, that the account of the origins
as it is given in Genesis cannot be isolated historically
speaking from the mythologies current at this period in
the Middle East. Now it was the Babylonian cosmogony
especially which at the time of Abraham was common all
over the valley of the Two Rivers and the land of Canaan.

134

From this fact we can be sure that the patriarch in his tent had often heard the recitation of an ancient Sumero-Akkadian poem called by Assyriologists *Enuma Elish* (from its first words which mean 'When on high').

This text, discovered in 1875, has come down to us on seven clay tablets. The version that we have dates from a period a little later than that of Abraham; it belongs to the time of Hammurabi (eighteenth century B.C.). But we know from other sources that this ancient legend was already current from the Persian Gulf to the banks of the Jordan for many centuries previously. In the form in which we have it, it is an account of the adventures of Marduk, god of Babylon, but it also provides us with curious details about the origins of the world, at least as the Sumero-Akkadians saw it. We know that this traditional poem *Enuma Elish* was extremely popular throughout ancient Mesopotamia. Modern scholarship believes that it had considerable influence on the intellectual activity of the Babylonians and Assyrians. For generations the scribes transcribed it on tablets of humid clay. It was read, it was recited at assemblies of the faithful, it was commented on and explained. In the schools of Akkad certain passages of it were set for amplification as an exercise in composition. In addition it was widely used in literature (which by definition remained always of a religious character). On certain festivals, especially at the New Year, it was solemnly recited; in its account of the creation a whole philosophy was inherent.

This religious epic is of considerable importance for our subject; Abraham must have listened to it time and again in a spirit of reverence. Thus a rapid examination of its literary content illustrated finally by certain Chaldaean and Egyptian contributions will be of assistance in our enquiry.

CHAOS: In the beginning there existed matter. It appeared in chaotic form in which the upper waters (the fresh water, *Apsu*) and the lower waters (the sea, the goddess *Tiamat*) were mingled. This chaos, Apsu-Tiamat, seemed to be eternal.

BIRTH OF THE YOUNG GODS: the combination Apsu-Tiamat gave birth to gods. Among these Marduk stands out as a dynamic and realist deity opposed to the prevailing chaos and its negative character. Thus the new generations began to upset Tiamat's rest; soon a sort of league was established which delegated to Marduk the task of imposing a new order of things.

THE STRUGGLE: Parricide becomes necessary. Marduk decides to kill the aged Tiamat and this will enable him to establish the new order. But Tiamat has resolved to defend herself and gives birth to eleven fearful monsters. Marduk, very courageously, does not hesitate to join battle. He makes an enormous net and proceeds to the creation of terrible winds intended to cause disturbance in Tiamat (the primitive liquid mass).

> And so the battle begins.
> Marduk stretches forth his net,
> He wraps it round Tiamat.
> He flings the bad winds at her face,
> Tiamat opens her mouth as wide as she can,
> Marduk makes the bad winds go in
> so that she cannot close her lips.
> Her heart turned upside down,
> she opened her mouth wide.
> With an arrow Marduk transfixes her,
> he cuts off her limbs, tears out her heart,
> reduces her to impotence and destroys her life.

CREATION OF HEAVEN AND EARTH: Marduk, the conquering hero, cuts up the corpse of Tiamat to make, as the cuneiform text informs us, 'a work of art'. He cuts the body into two portions 'like an oyster'. From one half of Tiamat he makes heaven, from the other he forms the earth which he distinguishes carefully from the 'lower waters'.

CREATION OF THE STARS: After this Marduk concerns himself with arranging a dwelling for the gods, new gods:

He established the stars which are their images.

He determined the year, he defined the seasons.

For the twelve months he established three stars.

He caused Sin [the moon] to shine and entrusted the night to her.

CREATION OF THE PLANTS AND ANIMALS: the poem then goes on to portray the creation, effected by Marduk, of Shamash (the divine Sun), then of the plants and animals; lastly, of man. The following is the summary of the operation according to the Chaldaean cosmogony:

The gods made the earth solid,

They produced the creatures of life,

the beasts of the fields, the domestic animals,

and they created the crowds of the cities.

CREATION OF MAN: Thus man appears, at the end of creation. All the cosmogonies of the Near East, whether they are Mesopotamian or Egyptian, place the emphasis in this event on a very special intervention of the deity. In the *Enuma Elish* the human being is moulded from potter's clay mixed with Tiamat's blood. In Egypt man is born from the tears of Osiris or comes to life at the fingers of Chnum, the potter-god with a ram's head, who shapes him from the mud of the Nile. Elsewhere he is the son of a goddess or a divine couple. Always the direct intervention of a supernatural being, or supernatural beings is required.

MAN'S ROLE IN CREATION: By giving life to men

the gods of the eastern pantheons followed a plan. Human beings were responsible for the worship of the deity; in addition, through sacrifices, burnt offerings and various gifts they provide for the food of the gods. For this good reason the gods generally take care to create several couples.

From this short sketch we can obtain an approximate idea of the legendary context and mythological climate on the subject of origins to which the patriarchs were accustomed; not only Abraham, but also the following generations of Hebrew shepherd chiefs — Isaac, Jacob and Joseph; not only the succession of nomad shepherd chiefs but also the Hebrew people right down to the exile in Babylon (586–538 B.C.).

And so the question arises: how and at what period did there appear in the Bible the account of the origins as it is given in the first chapter of Genesis. Even at the end of the period of the kings (900 B.C.), or when the pick of the Jews of Jerusalem were deported to Babylon on the orders of Nebuchadnezzar (586 B.C.), these Babylonian legends, summarized above, seem to have proved very attractive to the Israelites. When the Judaean colony, which was not uncultured, was brusquely transported to Babylon it came into contact with the Mesopotamian theory regarding the origin of the world. Babylon, it should be remembered was Marduk's city; he was its god and its protector. In other words, the *Enuma Elish* was recited, read and carried about.

At that time, it seems, a Hebrew priest of the sixth or fifth century went back to the old Yahwistic account, dating from the nomadic period, and adapted it more closely still to the usual account, favoured by the Babylonians, which had become fashionable again among the Israelite exiles in the central region of the Two Rivers.

138

It should be borne in mind, however, that the sacred writers who thus made use of oriental legends with which they were very well acquainted, took great care not to be contaminated by pagan doctrine. With remarkable single-mindedness they remained faithful to their noble and grandiose theology, a theology which was entirely based on the revelation of the One God.

This rapid sketch will have given some idea of what Abraham might have known about the creation of the world and of man.

Eden, or Paradise (Yahwistic account)

In the Bible Eden means an eastern desert country in which God planted a garden. *Edin,* in Sumerian, and *edinu* in Babylonian, means plain or steppe. In fact in the biblical narrative this garden, or Eden, appears as a sort of luxuriant oasis. Garden in Hebrew is *gan,* and in Greek *paradeisos,* which the Christians have made into Paradise.

Was there a religious tradition by which Abraham could have known of this garden of Paradise? Before answering this question, and to make what follows clearer, remember the three features of the biblical Eden.

In the centre there were two trees, clearly distinguished: the tree of life and the tree of knowledge. There was a river divided into four arms which watered the garden. After the sin committed by Adam and Eve Yahweh posted cherubs to prevent the human couple, who had lost their rights, from returning to the garden. Now we shall find these three elements, somewhat unexpectedly, in Mesopotamian works which are far earlier than Abraham. Some years ago André Parrot the Assyriologist discovered the ancient city of Mari, which was sacked by Hammurabi's soldiers in about 1700 B.C. And in the palace of Mari he managed to free from sand an extraordinary painting known as the 'investiture' which has the following features:

In the middle a god (or a goddess) holding to his chest a vessel from which gushes out a fourfold stream. That is a very ancient Babylonian theme, going back to the third millennium: that is to a period considerably earlier than Abraham's. Obviously we have here the 'four rivers' of the biblical description.

On each side of the central feature of the picture are two trees. One of them is too stylized to be identified. The other is a palm tree. We may well consider that these two trees correspond to the two of the biblical account.

Lastly, against the trees, and turned towards them, are three weird animals: these are the well-known *kerubim*, the sacred guardians of Mesopotamian palaces; they are also the cherubs of the Bible (Gen. 3: 24).

It is only right to admit that the Mari painting is not in every way identical with the biblical description of Eden. Thus the various elements of the picture are duplicated: there are in fact four trees, eight rivers. Archaeologists explain this by the Babylonians' pronounced taste for symmetry. In any case we are bound to acknowledge that in the Mari painting the established Sumero-Akkadian tradition is depicted, and we cannot doubt that Abraham in his day had knowledge, through the handing down of the legend, of the existence of a garden (*edinu*), planted with mysterious trees, watered by rivers and watched over by winged guardians, the *kerubim* of the Babylonians.

The Flood

In the first place we must briefly consider the composition of this narrative (Gen. 6–7). According to Fr Roland de Vaux, O.P., of the Ecole Biblique in Jerusalem, this section contains two parallel accounts: a Yahwistic

Cuneiform characters

narrative (J), full of life and colour, and a priestly narrative (P), more definite and thoughtful but also more succinct. [6] The final writer respected these two sources received from tradition, which agreed in substance; but he did not seek to get rid of differences of detail. [7]

On bricks from Mesopotamian libraries archaeologists have been able to make out various accounts of the flood, sacred narratives which form the fundamental elements of the religious literature of the land of the Two Rivers. At first glance the similarities of these Sumero-Akkadian

[6] The Yahwistic narrative given here by the Bible was certainly preceded by several written versions, reproducing oral versions of a much earlier date; it took form and was consigned to writing very probably at the time of King Solomon (970–931). The priestly narrative is nowadays regarded as being drawn up during the exile in Babylon (586–538); but it only took definitive form after the Return (538).

[7] The following differences may be noticed: In J the flood lasts forty days, and in the ark Noah took in seven pairs of clean animals and one pair of unclean animals. In P the flood lasts 150 days and Noah took with him only one pair of each kind 'having the breath of life'.

(and we have even a Sumerian text of very early date) with the story of Noah as it is given in the Bible, appears striking enough. But very quickly particular differences (of a spiritual nature) appear, distinguishing the Babylonian versions from the biblical account.

Thus the Mesopotamian epic describes a meeting of the gods. After a drunken orgy, for no reason at all they decide to destroy the human race. But one of the deities of this strange pantheon secretly came to warn a man called Uta-napishtim, telling him of the approaching catastrophe and advising him to build a boat on which he will be able to embark with his family and some of the beasts of the fields. At this point the storm occurs, the waters cover the whole of the earth, humanity is wiped out, with the exception of course of Uta-napishtim and his precious cargo.

The gods, much afraid of the terrible destruction they had wrought, took refuge 'in the heaven of Anu, crouching down like dogs', an odd attitude for supernatural beings.

Weeks passed. From a window of the ark Uta-napishtim released a dove which at the end of a certain space returned to the ark. A swallow was next released; this too returned. A little later a crow was let out; it did not return and from this it was inferred that it had found a piece of dry land where the floods had subsided. Shortly afterwards the ark touched land. Uta-napishtim then came out of the ark and offered a sacrifice of thanksgiving to the gods, who 'scented the sweet odour (of the burnt meat) and gathered like flies around the altar'.

The imposing biblical narrative is quite different in spirit. It shows us Yahweh, his patience exhausted by the wickedness of men and having come to the conclusion that indeed he can expect nothing of this primitive race

142

which is increasingly plunged in idolatry. As a result he decides to destroy all, save for one just man, Noah. With this patriarch and his family the Lord intends to begin creation over again, on a different basis: justice and mercy, punishment of evil, salvation granted to men whose hearts have remained pure.

Although the two versions, the Babylonian and the biblical, show some curious points of resemblance, the spirit inspiring them could not be more different. In the Mesopotamian account a rather sordid materialism seems to prevail. In that of Genesis there is an enlightened spirituality in which the principal lessons of applied morality appear.

The old Sumero-Akkadian theme of the Flood formed an integral part of the pagan beliefs brought from Ur to Canaan by the nomad shepherd Abraham. But later, in the course of centuries, at the period of the kings, and especially at that of the Exile, the archaic tradition of the Mesopotamian Flood was most probably revised and recast, to become, on a final analysis, a sort of moral tale.

The reader is probably aware that certain Assyriologists pride themselves on having discovered at the site of their excavations very clear traces of the Flood. In Lower Mesopotamia, in those cities in which the archaeologists have undertaken deep excavations, layers of alluvial earth have been discovered which are proof of an extensive flood. And certain specialists have not hesitated to hazard the opinion that we have here proof of the Flood.

It would be better, probably, to talk of floods in the plural; or, better still, of inundations by the river, which occurred locally at successive periods. Of course, as has just been pointed out, in certain cities there can be observed a river of mud now solidified, separating two civilizations of different dates. A catastrophic inundation

143

occurred and life could not continue in these places for a long time after the destructive invasion of the waters of the river.

But the dates of this Flood differ from city to city. And the Flood itself does not seem always to have happened with the same violence. Thus, between the flood of Ur (dated by Sir Leonard Woolley in 2800) and the flood of Kish (dated by Langdon in 3300) there is an interval of 500 years. At Nineveh the Flood occurred about 3800–3700. Further examples could be given: nowhere do the dates agree.

In the present state of our knowledge it would be wise to adopt conclusions like those of André Parrot, the Assyriologist: this flood, or rather the floods must be regarded merely as regional inundations due to the breaching of a dyke intended to retain as far as possible the waters of the river. The great variation in thickness of the layers of alluvial mud shows us that in one place the flooding must have been a dreadful tragedy, while in another elsewhere it was merely incidental. Consequently, it is not surprising to find that the dates of the various floods differ very considerably. Finally, it may be added that according to the geologists the overflowing of its banks by the Euphrates was never a generalized phenomenon.

On the other hand, it can be easily understood that these excessive floodings, often of a terrifying nature, should, with the help of an oriental imagination, have assumed the appearance of a worldwide catastrophe in which the whole of human-kind perished, always excepted, of course, the man in the boat with his family and his cargo of animals.

The Tower of Babel

Could the patriarch Abraham have known of the

144

construction and the whole story of the celebrated Tower? (Gen. 11: 1–9).

This is the biblical account of the occurrence. At this time, we are informed, *throughout the earth men spoke the same language, with the same vocabulary. Now as they moved eastwards they found a plain in the land of Shinar where they settled. They said to one another, 'come let us make bricks and bake them in the fire'. For stone they used bricks and for mortar they used bitumen.*[8] *'Come,' they said, 'let us build ourselves a town and a tower with its top reaching heaven. Let us make a name for ourselves, so that we may not be scattered about the whole earth.'* The sequel is known: to prevent men reaching heaven, Yahweh decided to confuse their language. Since they no longer understood each other the builders were obliged to call a halt to their work. This city in which a beginning had been made on building the tower in the Bible is called Babel.[9]

Historians are inclined to think that this Hebrew tradition is probably a reflection of impressions received by the nomad shepherds who, leading their flocks over the steppes at some distance from the cities could, on occasion, make out on the horizon the heavy, darkening mass of the ziggurats, often more or less in ruins, and certainly in a dilapidated condition as a consequence of the military invasions of the Elamite and other barbarians. The Hebrew shepherds explained the enormous buildings by the pride and folly of the men of the cities who had planned to climb up to heaven to dislodge Yahweh from

[8] This was a typically Sumerian way of building, and very different from the architectural ideas of the Hebrews. They were to live in tents until after their return from Egypt and the conquest of the land of Canaan under the guidance of Joshua (about 1220 B.C.).

[9] This was the ziggurat of Babylon. In Akkadian Bab-Ilu means the gate of God. It seems that the biblical scribe wanted to make a pun on the root *ell* which signifies 'confuse'. The joke does not work. It is Bab-Ilu the Gate of God which gave its name to Babylon.

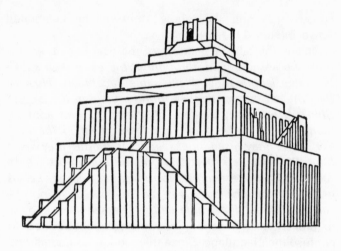

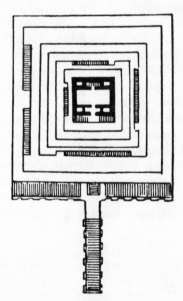

Reconstruction of the 'Tower of Babel' (Busink)

it. In fact, heaven was the name that the Babylonians gave to the *cella* of the god established at the highest and last platform of the monument. From that we can see the misunderstanding on the part of the nomads. They could only be deeply impressed when faced with this lofty architecture which seemed to them to be a defiance of the deity.

Summary

It seems doubtful that Abraham could have known of the account of the creation as it can be read nowadays in the first pages of Genesis. We have seen that the passages as we now have them must be dated from the sixth or fifth centuries B.C., that is, from a period later than Abraham's by a millennium and a half. In fact he could only have had an idea of the origins of the universe and of man through the legendary explanations of the Babylonian poem *Enuma Elish*.

Eden, the garden: by reason of certain material analogies between the Babylonian tradition and the paradise of the Bible we can conclude that Abraham certainly possessed some idea of the *Edinu* of Mesopotamian theology.

The Flood: the numerous cuneiform accounts of the catastrophy enable us to think that the narrative of the great Flood was known throughout the whole of the Valley of the Two Rivers. Abraham could not have been unaware of it, at least in its Mesopotamian form.

The Tower of Babel: in the eyes of the Hebrew shepherds feeding their flocks of sheep on the steppes the ziggurat often appeared as a sacrilegious image: a work of inordinate pride, a proof of the spiritual perversion of the idolaters. The builders of these colossal constructions wished to reach God (that was at any rate the explanation of the nomads) by means of a material work.

The end of a cycle

From Haran to Shechem, from Shechem to Bethel, from Bethel to Hebron, Abraham seems to have gone through the theological cycle whence were to emerge, later, orthodox Judaism and then Christianity. Abraham's period concludes at Hebron under the Oak of Mamre. But the patriarch's wanderings were not yet over. There were to be further adventures in which Yahweh also figured.

6

FAMILY AFFAIRS

Again on two different occasions Abraham would encounter God, but in fact we have come to an end of the main series of revelations of the supreme being to the former shepherd of Ur. The explanation for this is simple: the promise has been given and then confirmed; the Covenant promulgated during a solemn ceremony has in its turn been confirmed also. In addition, Abraham has been told that in a short while a son will be born to him according to the flesh. After which the nomad chieftain, with great simplicity, continued his normal existence as a wandering shepherd.

Lot and his daughters: a shameful incident
(Gen. 19: 30–80)

After the disaster which destroyed Sodom, Gomorrah, Admah and Zeboiim in the valley of Siddim, Abraham's nephew, the patriarch Lot, sought refuge in the city of Zoar. Owing to the presence of this just man within its walls Zoar was spared from destruction by fire.

Now shortly after these dramatic events Genesis states that Lot decided to settle in the hill country, probably to the east of the Dead Sea, the modern Jordan. During their flight his wife encountered a fearful death under a shower of brimstone, so that Lot had with him only his two daughters. In this isolated part of the country there was no man for them to marry and so continue the line.

And so it appeared that Lot's family would die out. To the eastern mentality no more lamentable social or religious catastrophe could be imagined. But the two daughters quickly found the solution to the problem. They resolved to make their father drunk and, taking advantage of his condition, sleep with him in turn. Thus they became pregnant and in due time produced two sons. One of them was named Moab, who was to become the ancestor of the Moabites; the other was called Ben-ammi, from whom descended the Bene-ammon, or Ammonites.

There is an historical explanation of this story. The Moabites and Ammonites gloried in their descent from Abraham through Lot, though the question of incest naturally was not raised. On the other hand, the biblical scribe responsible for the inclusion of this episode was writing in the sixth or fifth century B.C., at a time when Moabites and Ammonites had become the declared enemies of Israel. It may well be, consequently, that the writer seized the opportunity to slander the two military and political opponents of his country. Incest was held in horror by the Israelites and, indeed, by the Assyro-Babylonians. The Mesopotamian code of Hammurabi was very clear on this point and punished by death any such injury to social morality. Thus the rather doubtful story of Lot's daughters can probably be explained as a calumny perpetrated at a later date (at least a millennium after the event).

Abraham, Sarah and Abimelech, king of Gerar

Once more a change of pasture was necessary; Abraham left Hebron and set out towards the Negeb. Then he returned by way of Gerar, the domain of Abimelech, the petty king of the region.

Family Affairs

Here Abraham repeated the trick that previously he played on Pharaoh when he settled in Egypt. Once again, to avoid harsh treatment at the hands of the authorities of the country, Abraham declared that Sarah was not his wife but his sister. As on arrival in Egypt, Sarah, directly they entered Gerar, was noticed by the king's men and shortly afterwards was on her way to the royal harem. But God warned Abimelech in a dream that Sarah was married, and ordered him to send her back at once to her husband. Abimelech hastened to return Sarah to Abraham, giving him at the same time 'sheep, cattle, men and women slaves'. To Sarah he said 'I am giving one thousand pieces of silver to your brother' (since after all he was her brother).

It must be said at once, and this is the opinion of orthodox commentators, that this repetition of the Egyptian episode must be regarded as a 'doublet'. The Egyptian account was of Yahwistic origin. This one belongs to the Elohistic cycle. This doublet is repeated again in Gen. 26; on this occasion it is Isaac (Abraham's son) and his wife Rebekah who are the actors; once more it occurs at Gerar and during the time of the king Abimelech. It seems that this little detail struck the story-tellers and their audience the shepherds as so amusing that it was repeated on three occasions. It is noticeable that this Elohistic doublet fits very awkwardly into the main Yahwistic narrative which forms its setting. Sarah, as we know, had then reached an advanced age; she had laughed when Yahweh announced the birth of Isaac, declaring that she was past the age of child-bearing and that she had grown old. Her admission to Abimelech's harem seems a little difficult to imagine. This then is a doublet rather awkwardly inserted into the text.

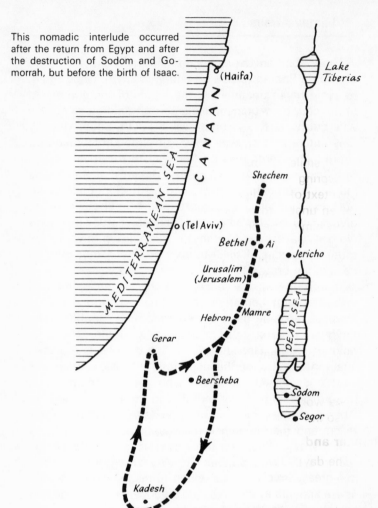

This nomadic interlude occurred after the return from Egypt and after the destruction of Sodom and Gomorrah, but before the birth of Isaac.

(Haifa)

Lake Tiberias

C A N A A N

Shechem

o (Tel Aviv)

MEDITERRANEAN SEA

Bethel ● ● *Ai*

● *Jericho*

Urusalim (Jerusalem)

Hebron ● *Mamre*

DEAD SEA

Gerar

● *Beersheba*

● *Sodom*

● *Segor*

Kadesh

1. Abraham's clan of shepherds left Hebron (The Oak of Mamre) to make the journey round the Negeb. But there was no question this time of going so far as Egypt.

2. On arrival at the south of the Oasis of Kadesh Abraham and his flocks returned towards the north in the direction of Gerar. Here occurred the incidents between Abimelech and Abraham.

3. From Gerar he returned by way of Beersheba to the camp at Mamre (Hebron).

Isaac the child of the promise

At the time foretold by Yahweh when he appeared at the Oak of Mamre, that is, a year after the strange visit of the unknown man accompanied by his two servants, Sarah, despite her age, gave birth to Isaac. The name Isaac is a shortened form of the expression Ishq-El meaning 'may God smile' or 'may God be kind'. With this unexpected offspring of the patriarch we are undoubtedly in the context of laughter, or at least of smiling. Abraham had been unable to prevent himself laughing when Yahweh told him of the coming birth of an heir. Later at the Oak of Mamre, hearing the prophecy promising her a son despite her great age, Sarah in her unbelief laughed also. But the laughter was not yet finished. Shortly after the birth of this miracle-child Sarah exclaimed: *'God has given me cause to laugh; all those who hear of it will laugh with me.'* Isaac, 'may God smile', seems to have pleased both Yahwistic and Elohistic writers who are fond of repeating this play on words in which the oriental mind once more shows us its marked taste for puns. So Sarah's child had been born, the child of the free woman. But it must not be forgotten that there was also in Abraham's tent a child of Hagar, the slave girl.

Hagar and her son Ishmael dismissed (Gen. 21: 8–20)

The day on which the child Isaac was weaned was one of great rejoicing. And it was general except for Sarah who appears always to have been quick to take offence; she had no room in her heart for the Egyptian concubine whom nevertheless she herself had chosen for her husband, and who some years previously had given birth to Ishmael. Delaying no longer, Sarah informed Abraham of her feelings and suggested to him the decision that ought to be taken: *'Drive away that slave girl and her son, this slave girl's son is not to share the inheritance with my son Isaac.'* And the Bible adds *this greatly distressed Abraham because of his son*.

Previously, Sarah had behaved so harshly towards Hagar the Egyptian, when she was pregnant before the birth of Ishmael, that in peril of her life she had fled to the desert. But on Yahweh's advice she had soon returned to the camp. In these somewhat dramatic circumstances Abraham seems to have said nothing about the harsh treatment which his legitimate wife meted out to his concubine, then soon to give birth to Ishmael. But now, when Sarah proposed to banish Hagar and her son to the desert, we find Abraham hesitating, unable to decide. Almost it seems he rebelled. What is the explanation of these two different ways of reacting to events which were very similar? The reason for it is that Abraham here is acting in accordance with Sumerian law. So long as a concubine had no children, according to this law, she retained her status as a slave, and so was subject to the legitimate wife. If the slave-concubine took it into her head to act as a rival to her mistress the latter could get rid of her as she liked. In her ill-treatment of Hagar, who had not yet given birth but was already pregnant, by compelling her, through continual scolding, in very desperation to flee to the desert, Sarah remained entirely within the law. Abraham, when questioned by Sarah about the differences which had arisen between the two women, answered his wife, saying of the slave-concubine: *Your slave girl is at your disposal, treat her as you think fit* (Gen. 16: 6). This of course was all quite legal at the time, but now Sarah seemed on the point of doing something illegal. She began by asking Abraham to drive Hagar and her son out of the tribe, so that Ishmael would be deprived of his legitimate rights of inheritance after the patriarch's death. Such an action would have been in plain contradiction to the articles of the Mesopotamian code. Sarah spoke in the heat of the moment. Abraham, however, was well aware of the law and we have a clear picture of the patriarch's embarrassment when his wife asked him to act in violation of the law and against justice. Ishmael indeed, we must not forget, was the child who had been properly legitimized by the fact that his birth took place under special circumstances. Sarah's Egyptian slave gave birth 'on the lap' of the wife; legally speaking he thereby became Sarah's son. Consequently, in regard to the succession, he was Isaac's equal in every way.

In this case, to cut him off with no indemnity whatever would have been a formal infraction of the law of Ur which Abraham had come to know during his time in the delta region of the Euphrates. It can be understood therefore why it required the express order of Yahweh for the patriarch to accede to the request of his wife. Unexpectedly God intervened in this family matter to give a decision which at first sight, at least, seems somewhat unexpected. *Do not distress yourself on account of the boy and your slave girl,* said Yahweh. *Grant Sarah all she asks of you, for it is through Isaac that your name will be carried on. But the slave girl's son I will also make into a nation, for he is your child too* (Gen. 21: 2–13).

Thus God announced his plan. It was necessary, no doubt, for the internal formation of the Chosen People that Isaac, the son of the free woman, the child of pure Hebrew blood, should stand alone at the origin of the Israelite community. 'Do not distress yourself on account of the boy': God had spoken. Abraham, always faithful, always placing his entire trust in the words of the Lord, obeyed in all simplicity.

Then occurred the dramatic action, so simple in its literary expression and yet so powerfully described that

155

in reading it we almost feel that we are eye witnesses. *Rising early next morning Abraham took some bread and a skin of water and, giving them to Hagar, he put the child on her shoulder and sent her away. Hagar,* the Bible tells us, *wandered off into the wilderness of Beersheba.* A glance at the map shows that this oasis is on the edge of the Negeb, a desolate, unfriendly, savage and uncultivated region, a land of thirst or even of death for the solitary traveller without provisions or the means to make a camp, walking over the sand or the stony steppe.

Such an expedition could not go on for very long. *When the skin of water was finished she abandoned the child under a bush. Then she went and sat down at a distance, about a bow shot away, saying to herself, 'I cannot see the child die'. So she sat at a distance and the child wailed and wept* (Gen. 21: 15–16). Sarah's plan seemed about to succeed, but God comforted Hagar: *'Do not be afraid, for God has heard* [1] *the boy's cry where he lies. Come, pick up the boy and hold him safe, for I will make him into a great nation.' Then God opened Hagar's eyes and she saw a well, so she went and filled the skin with water and gave the boy a drink* (Gen. 21: 17–19). Thus for the moment they were saved.

As he had promised to Abraham God watched over the mother and child. The latter grew up and remained in the desert and became a bowman. He made his home in the wilderness of Paran [2] and his mother chose him a wife from Egypt. [3]

After this we hear little more of Ishmael, at least in the

[1] Another play on words in a proper name; *Ishma el* means, in fact, 'may God hear'.

[2] The desert of Paran (or Pharan) is situated in the north-western part of the peninsula of Sinai at about 125 miles from the oasis of Beersheba.

[3] For the second time, thus, Ishmael's Egyptian blood was mixed with Hebrew blood. From this twofold origin, according to oriental tradition, were to spring the Ishmaelite Arabs, who shared the characteristics of both peoples.

156

Bible. We may well imagine that the two lonely figures were picked up and accepted by another wandering clan in the wilderness of Sinai. Ishmael appears for the last time, on this occasion at the side of his half brother Isaac, at the burial of his father Abraham in the cave of Machpelah.

At the well of Beersheba

The scene depicted for us in the Bible at the well of Beersheba (Gen. 21: 25–33) is typical of nomad life; it holds no very great interest for us in itself but provides a revealing sidelight on the hard lives of the Hebrew shepherds.

Abraham and his flocks were still in the territory of Abimelech, king of Gerar. There had been a quarrel between Abimelech's and Abraham's shepherds, hardly surprising in the circumstances, over a well belonging to the latter, that is, one which had been sunk by his men. To settle the affair Abimelech came to see Abraham and very fairly acknowledged the wrongs committed by his men. Upon this the two chiefs resolved to swear a mutual oath of peace. Abraham, who at the time was leading his flocks over Abimelech's territory, offered the king a certain number of sheep and cattle (it was a normal tribute in the circumstances). After this, as a sort of supplementary guarantee to the pact of friendship, Abraham asked Abimelech to accept from him seven lambs. *'You must accept these seven lambs from me,'* explained Abraham, *'as evidence that I have dug this well.'* That is why this place was called Beersheba – *Beer Sheba* in Hebrew means the 'well of the oath'. When Abimelech left, Abraham planted a tamarisk at Beersheba and there invoked Yahweh, 'the everlasting God'.

This well at Beersheba is an important place in the lives of the great patriarchs, Abraham, Isaac and Jacob;

The more laborious tasks at the well are left to the women

it is surrounded by the little oasis to which it gave rise, and is situated in the wilderness of Negeb some twenty-four miles south-west of Hebron. At Hebron there is the grassy mountain land of Judaea, but in the wilderness of Beersheba to reach the oasis means crossing dreadful land strewn with yellowish grey limestone boulders with here and there, a few spindly oaks and arbutus. In spring the sparse vegetation consists of broom and milk-vetch, iris and anemones, scarcely sufficient to feed the flocks of sheep as they are led step by step by their shepherds over the desolate ground. For a reasonably normal life, plants, animals and men must find shelter round the wells.

Ever since the time of the patriarchs the wells have been renowned for the abundance and excellent quality of their water. There are two in particular at about a hundred yards from each other on the north bank of the wadi es-Seba which appear to have been arranged for watering sheep. Both are circular and their inside walls are built with regularly shaped stones. The larger of the two is twelve feet in diameter and the water, according to the time of year, is at a depth of between forty and fifty feet. The other is smaller but is of the same depth. The antiquity of these wells is shown by the marks on the stones which were deeply hollowed and scored by the hempen ropes in pulling up the buckets. In a semi-circle round the wells stand the stone or earthenware troughs which the patriarchs' shepherds used to fill with water for their beasts. Even nowadays camel drivers and shepherds arrive at the end of the day in this same place to carry out the same task, performing the same centuries old actions.

The sacrifice of Isaac (Gen. 22)

It seems indeed as if Yahweh had heaped kindnesses upon Abraham — repeated promises, the assurance confirmed on several occasions of an immense posterity, repeated blessings; he seemed to lack nothing, for the moment. Abraham had benefitted by the loftiest spiritual revelations and, indeed, material blessings of the most desirable kind for a just and wise man.

And now quite unexpectedly he had to undergo a formidable trial. There is nothing surprising in this, for as history tells us those chosen by God at certain times undergo moral sufferings which seem destined, at least from the human point of view, to take the measure of the soul, to weigh its spiritual worth; to determine, in short, whether the person in question is equal to the super-human task awaiting him.

There came the summons from the Most High, *'Abraham, Abraham!' 'Here I am,'* Abraham replied. Thereupon the Lord gave him a terrible and entirely unforeseen order: *'Take your son, your only child Isaac, whom you love, and go to the land of Moriah. There you shall offer him as a burnt offering, on a mountain I will point out to you'* (Gen. 22: 2).

Human sacrifice is a novel and strange idea occurring here in the biblical narrative. Where did it come from? From Sumer, Abraham's country of origin, or from Canaan where for many years now his flocks and people had been leading a wandering life?

It does not appear that the Sumerians of the valley of the Euphrates ever practised the horrible ceremonies during which a human being was put to death in honour of one or other of their deities. On leaving Ur Abraham took with him a number of Sumerian religious traditions and Akkadian legends but he certainly did not obtain from this Mesopotamian civilization the notion of ritual murder.

In modern times historical research and archaeological discoveries enable us to see the problem more clearly.

We know that human sacrifice was practised in the polytheistic religion of the land of Canaan. Moreover, even before the arrival of the Canaanites in the region bordering the Mediterranean (and this occurred in about 3000 B.C.), the native inhabitants practised such rites.

It is important to emphasize here that it was sacrifice of the first born that appears to have been especially common. The Phoenicians of Canaan jealously preserved in their colonies and Sicilian trading posts this religious practice of sacrificing the first-born of a family to one of the gods of their pantheon. And this continued until a fairly late period.

In the southern part of the land of Canaan (modern Palestine) archaeologists have found proof of these quasi-systematic massacres of the first-born. Thus at Gezer excavations have unearthed a considerable number of earthenware jars. In each of them was the skeleton of a child whose age seems not to have exceeded eight days. The victim had been suffocated in the jar itself, as appeared from the fact that fine earth had been packed around it and above it.

In the Canaanite rite sacrifice of the first-born seems to have been the rule. The reason for the practice was this: just as the first-fruits of the fields and the first offspring of an animal, born on the farm, were burnt on the altar, so the first child of a woman also 'belonged' to the god, the owner of the soil and the ruler of all life in his domain. By this offering, so painful for the parents, it was hoped to obtain from the god to whom the sacrifice was offered full protection and many blessings.

Of course, not all the bones of children that have been unearthed can be regarded as the result of sacrificial offerings. The archaeologists have sometimes been a little hasty in their generalizations. It should be added that occasionally (and this has been confirmed by

161

excavation) the child to be sacrificed was replaced by a substitute victim – a lamb, a pigeon, or a kid. And at an early date the cruel rite was reduced to this 'redeeming' of the human victim by substituting a sacrificial animal.

These were the ideas on the putting to death of a child, whether new born or adolescent, accepted in the Canaanite cities near the steppes where Abraham grazed his flocks, at the time when Yahweh gave him the order to sacrifice his son, his 'only' son, Isaac, as the Bible says (and he could correctly so be called since the casting out of Ishmael), the son of his old age, the offspring on whom the promise rested.

Rising early next morning Abraham saddled his ass (Gen. 23: 3). The ass, the beast best suited for this kind of journey of moderate length, is reddish brown in colour and higher and more solidly built than its European cousin. It is capable of going at the same, unflagging pace, almost without stopping from dawn until dusk. And in stony country it is very surefooted for its long hooves are hollow with sharp edges. In ancient times of course there were no metal shoes. The saddle mentioned was just a blanket kept in place by a belly-band. A curious detail is provided by some Egyptian representations, especially that of the scribe Urchu (fifth dynasty) astride his mount, which show the ass with its master on it, preceded by a slave with a cudgel, and followed by a second with another cudgel. It can only be supposed that the ass of the Near East, like its European cousin, required a certain amount of exhortation to make it proceed. That is probably the explanation of the two servants accompanying Abraham sitting on his beast while Isaac, with great respect, went on foot beside his father. Before leaving Abraham *took the wood for the burnt offering*; dry boughs for burning the body might not be found on arrival.

For three days the expedition travelled towards Moriah, the land designated by God as the destination of this strange journey. He had clearly stated the place of sacrifice – *'on a mountain I will point out to you'*. Obviously the Israelites would be concerned to know the geographical situation of this place. The author of Chronicles identifies Moriah with the rock where later (about 967 B.C.) King Solomon was to build the Temple of Jerusalem. The trouble is that the Book of Chronicles is of relatively recent composition. All the same this tradition has been accepted for thousands of years, but nowadays Hebrew scholars show considerable reserve in identifying this place.

Abraham called his men to a halt at the foot of the mountain, and ordered his servants to remain there until his return; carrying in his own hands the fire and the knife he began the ascent of the slope. The wood for the burnt offering he loaded on Isaac's shoulders. Symbolist commentators have pointed to the parallel between the material circumstances of this sacrifice and that other one which was to take place eighteen hundred years after these events, namely, our Lord's going up to Calvary carrying on his shoulders the wood of the cross, the wood intended for his own sacrifice.

Surprised by these mysterious preparations *Isaac spoke to his father Abraham, 'Father,' he said. 'Yes, my son,' he replied. 'Look,' he said, 'here are the fire and the wood, but where is the lamb for the burnt offering?' Abraham answered, 'My son, God himself will provide the lamb for the burnt offering.' Then the two of them went on together* (Gen. 22: 7).

After building an altar, a rudimentary affair no doubt, made of two or three large stones piled together, Abraham made ready the wood on top of this altar. Then he bound his son, but just as he 'stretched out his hand

and seized the knife to kill his son' God intervened to give a different and unexpected turn to the event: *the angel of Yahweh called to him from heaven. 'Abraham, Abraham,' he said. 'I am here,' he replied. 'Do not raise your hand against the boy,' the angel said. 'Do not harm him for now I know you fear God. You have not refused me your son, your only son.'* At this moment Abraham saw near the altar a ram, caught by its horns in a bush, unable to free itself. He at once understood that this beast had been sent by the Most High as a substitute victim. So he sacrificed it as a burnt offering instead and in place of his son.

At once God informed his faithful servant of the reward for his heroic obedience, unwavering faith and complete generosity. He renewed the promises, but there was one new feature: *'I swear by my own self — it is Yahweh who speaks. . . .'* That was the highest form of guarantee, God's oath. But notice that all the spiritual gifts from which Abraham benefitted hitherto must be regarded as gratuitous, and the testimony of heavenly goodwill. Now, after the dramatic events on Mount Moriah, Yahweh appears to bind himself by a kind of contract which is no longer strictly speaking unilateral. *'Because you have done this* [as a return for your obedience] *I will shower blessings upon you.'* The sacrifice of Isaac, prevented just in time, appears as the source of very great graces for the patriarch and his descendants.

'All the nations of the earth shall bless themselves by your descendants, as a reward for your obedience.' Through the patriarch's faith, the dramatic event of Moriah opens the way for the history of the Chosen People. Henceforward there is open to man the path whereby he could rise from the depths of polytheist materialism. The sacrifice of Isaac, halted at the last

moment, was to show the way to a slow ascent towards another sacrifice, a sacrifice which this time was to go on to the end, for there would be no ram to take the place of the victim, who indeed was irreplaceable. This was the sacrifice which took place eighteen hundred years after the scene on Moriah which for Christians is the pre-figuring of the tragedy of Golgotha.

On coming down from Moriah, accompanied by his son, Abraham found his servants awaiting him. The small party set out again for Beersheba where for the time being the camp was established.

Sarah's burial

Sarah died at Kiriath-arba, or Hebron, in the land of Canaan, and Abraham went in to mourn and grieve for her (Gen. 23: 2).

From Beersheba the clan moved on to Hebron, to the site of the former camp that we have already encountered under the oaks. It was there that Sarah died. The fifth-century scribe says little about the funeral rites on this occasion. Nevertheless, with the help of various details scattered about in other chapters of the Bible, it is possible to reconstitute the various phases of that day.

Directly Sarah had breathed her last they closed her eyes as tradition required (Gen. 46: 4); this was done to prevent the soul of the dead person leaving the body and going to prowl dangerously among the living. This action, which as a modern custom is a matter of reverence and devotion, can certainly be explained as a precautionary measure going back to the known origins of humanity; it is to be found in most funeral rites.

Then Abraham tenderly kissed his dead wife. Next, according to custom, the body of the dead woman was dressed in her finest clothes. *Abraham,* we are told, *went in to mourn and grieve for her.* In other words the lamentations began (Jer. 22: 18; Eccles. 12: 5). To carry out this necessary and noisy function the mourning women were already at their post.

You, there! Call the mourning women! Let them come!
Send for those who are best at it! Let them come!
Let them lose no time in raising the lament for us!
Let our eyes rain tears,
our eyelids run in weeping! (Jer. 9: 16–17.)

In the tent the widower remains prostrate before the funeral bier, though this does not prevent his receiving, in deep silence, the visit of relations and friends. To show his sorrow from time to time he may throw himself on the ground (Job 1: 20).

Directly death was observed to have taken place Abraham hastened to tear his clothes. The intention was to render oneself unrecognizable to the spirit of the dead wife, for at once after death it might attach itself to objects still in its memory. Moreover, for greater safety the funeral rite required that as soon as possible the tunic should be changed for the coarse garment known as the *saq*, made from woven goats' hair. It was a kind of loin-cloth which men and women tied round their waist at times of great sorrow, whether personal or national (Joel 1: 8; Jer. 49: 3). As a rule this hair garment was worn next to the skin with or without clothes over it. It was kept on during the night, when it took the place of a blanket. At a later period people were satisfied to wear the *saq* over the tunic, which was much less uncomfortable.

For the same purpose of setting a barrier between the dead person and the living it was customary to veil the face, and even to roll on the ground, to scatter ashes over the head and to shave off beard and hair. In addition, care was taken to place the hand in front of the mouth and nose so that the soul of the dead person could not penetrate the living body. And to prevent the spirit of the dead recognizing a living person it was custom to disfigure oneself by cuts on the face, though this practice was later forbidden by the Law (Deut. 14: 1).

All these customs seem to us like the remote echo of an age-old tradition, or the atavistic memory of a very ancient time in which, among the primitive Semites, the spirits of the dead were regarded as harmful, or at least somewhat dangerous, against which a man had to defend himself by certain precautions. But with time and spiritual progress some of these rites had gradually changed and, well before Abraham's time, they had been transformed into a propitiatory ceremonial.

The climate of the Near East, especially in summer, did not allow of a body being kept for very long in the tent. Generally, within eight hours after decease, the corpse was solemnly taken to its last resting place. It was urgently necessary, therefore, to bury Sarah. Abraham at once set about finding a suitable place for his wife's tomb.

Among all the Semites the burning of bodies was regarded as a profanation. Unlike what was later the rule among the Greeks and the Romans cremation was forbidden among the Hebrews just as it still is nowadays among the Arabs. And so Abraham sought a suitable place for burial. The nomad shepherds, wandering from one pasture to another, did not own any land at all, so that in the circumstances it was necessary to acquire as soon as possible a corner of a field, a piece of ground to be used as a grave, and indeed a family grave. Abraham had already noticed a cave in the neighbourhood of Hebron, a cave known as Machpelah. But why a cave? In the limestone massif, which forms almost the whole of the mountain region of Judaea, underground rivers had hollowed out numerous caverns, which bore every sign of being suitable for transformation into funeral vaults where, in time to come, the dead of the same family could find a resting place.

For Sarah's funeral the whole of the little village of Hebron, and all the farmers of the neighbourhood, had gathered at the gate of Hebron a short distance from the tents of the Hebrew clan. These peasant owners of the fields are called in the Bible the 'sons of Heth', that is, the Hittites. This is probably an anachronism, for it is known nowadays that in Abraham's time the Hittites did not yet constitute an ethnic group in the south of Palestine. It is probable that the small tribe here designated was formed of the Hurrites, a non-Semitic people.

Abraham went towards the group of landed proprietors standing before the gate of Hebron and spoke to them in typically oriental style: *'I am a stranger and settler among you,' he said. 'Let me own a burial-plot among you, so that I may take my dead wife and bury her.' The sons of Heth answered Abraham, 'Listen, my Lord, you are God's prince amongst us; bury your dead in the best of our tombs; not one of us would refuse you his tomb and keep you from burying your dead'* (Gen. 23: 4–6). So polite an answer hardly satisfied Abraham. Since the land of Canaan, by divine promise, was in process of becoming Abraham's own, the patriarch felt obliged to show proof of his taking possession; he felt it absolutely necessary to establish somewhere in the Promised Land (and why not in Hebron?) a holy place where his descendants would be able to gather together during their earthly existence, but also and more especially after their death. In short, he felt it important to obtain a valid title of ownership to that part of the land where he had camped for so long.

168

Abraham continued: *'If you are willing for me to take my dead wife and bury her, then listen to me. Intercede for me with Ephron, Zohar's son, to give me the cave he owns at Machpelah, which is on the edge of his land. Let him make it over to me in your presence at its full price, for me to own as a burial plot.'* There now took place a typical piece of oriental bargaining. Ephron, the owner of the cave, happened to be present; he at once replied to Abraham's request: *'I give you the land and I give you the cave on it; I make this gift in the sight of the sons of my people.* [4] *Bury your dead.'* Abraham answered: *'I will pay the price of the land; accept it from me and I will bury my dead there.'* Ephron answered Abraham, *'My Lord, listen to me. A property worth four hundred shekels of silver, what is a little thing like that between me and you? Bury your dead.'* Abraham agreed to Ephron's terms, and Abraham weighed [5] out for Ephron the silver he had stipulated in the hearing of the sons of Heth, namely four hundred shekels of silver, according to the current commercial rate.* This was according to local custom. Still nowadays in the shop of a Palestine antique dealer, if he has retained the old and noble traditions of his ancestors, a European buyer will be told on asking the price of an object: 'Take it for nothing, I give it to you!' Of course it is not to be believed. Courtesy requires that the customer should refuse, and then insist on a price being fixed. It is proper for the merchant to hesitate and evade the issue for a time. Finally, pressed by the buyer he mutters, 'Twenty dollars, what is that between you and me?' It is understood; the customer pays the sum and leaves with the purchase. *'Thus Ephron's field*

---

[4] Babylonian law is very clear on this point; the code of Hammurabi lays down that 'If anyone proceeds to a sale without witnesses or a contract, he is a thief and will be put to death.'

[5] There was no minted money, no coins were struck at this period: the ingots of gold or silver used in transactions were weighed. The shekel was the unit of weight in Israel. Four hundred shekels weighed about 156 ozs.

*at Machpelah opposite Mamre, the field and the cave
that was on it, and all the trees that were on it,* [6] *the whole
of its extent in every direction, passed into Abraham's
possession in the sight of the sons of Heth and of all the
citizens of the town. . . . And so the field and the cave
that was on it passed from the sons of Heth into Abraham's possession to be owned as a burial-plot'* (Gen.
23: 17–20).

Thus Abraham became a land owner. This forms a
turning point in the history of the Chosen People, for the
cave of Machpelah is the first plot, acquired in due form,
of the Promised Land.

Sarah's body was solemnly transported to the tomb in
the cave. It was not embalmed nor was there a sarco-
phagus in the Egyptian fashion. Possibly, in accordance
with the Mesopotamian custom, the body was wrapped
in a reed mat or, following the usage of the Aramean
shepherds, in a sheepskin. It was laid on a stone bench
carved out of the rock of the inner cave. Custom required
that the corpse should lie on its left side with the knees
drawn up towards the chin, the position of a child in the
mother's womb.

By analogy with the various tombs of the same period,
of which it has been possible to make an archaeological
study, it can be asserted with some probability that beside
Sarah's mortal remains Abraham had laid some small
jars, probably filled with water and very similar to those
used for fetching water from the well. In addition, almost
certainly there were vessels containing food, and also
stone knives. But all these various articles would be
intentionally broken or pierced, or rendered useless in

---

[6] 'The trees that were on it.' In a properly drawn up Mesopotamian contract
of sale it was very carefully specified that the trees were sold with the land. For
with the litigious spirit characteristic of the area the seller might argue that he
had sold the land but not the orchard planted on it, and in these circumstances
he could demand the crop produced by these trees.

some way: it was 'dead' funeral furniture because it was intended to accompany a dead person.

All this leads naturally to the question of what the first Hebrews thought about life after death. There should be no cause for surprise at the primitive nature of their ideas, which at that remote period were still clouded by the polytheistic beliefs with which Abraham's clan remained imbued. In fact, the patriarchs seem to have adopted two contradictory views of the future life. There were two dwellings accepted for the person after death; one was in Sheol, the other in the tomb.

Sheol is the place of the departed spirits. They live there with the same features as at the time of their death and with their earthly personality. But they have become *elohim,* that is, not gods indeed, but at least beings endowed with superhuman power and knowledge. Among the Hebrews of Abraham's time, as among the contemporaries of Isaac and Jacob (the second and third patriarchal generations), belief in a reward beyond the tomb cannot yet be discerned; this idea was only accepted in the second century B.C.

While admitting the gathering of the departed in Sheol the Hebrew shepherds thought that the dead person continued to enjoy a sort of slowed down existence in the tomb. They believed that the dead retained their own feelings and knowledge. From this arose the importance of burial, enabling the dead person to enjoy quiet and calm in the privacy of the tomb.

When Sarah's body had been laid upon the bench in the cave the entrance was closed with a huge boulder. It is difficult to say how long the mourning for Sarah continued, since the Bible gives different numbers of days according to the periods and the persons concerned. Thus there were seventy days for Jacob, thirty days for Moses and also for Aaron. Subsequently the seven days of mourning which followed the death of Saul seem to have become the rule, but for a father or mother the period of thirty days was retained. Very often widows, of their own free will, remained in mourning for the rest of their lives. In any case during the seven days following the death the mourner was forbidden to wash, shave, anoint his body with oil, wear anything on his feet (it was necessary to go barefoot) or to cover his head; and all the relatives of the dead person wore the *saq*.

On return from the cave of Machpelah, once the burial was over, Abraham and his near relatives were obliged to perform a ceremony of purification, since to have touched or even to have looked at a corpse was a cause of uncleanness. The tent also became unclean together with all those who had gone into the place in which the dead person lay. Seven days of special rites were required for those present to regain their previous state of cleanness.

Abraham was taken back to the camp by his family. He was still fasting and would continue to do so until sunset. At that moment friends, not members of the clan, would come to bring, from outside, the funeral meal. There could be no question in such circumstances of eating food from the camp since it would be considered unclean owing to the recent presence of the corpse. The friends urged the mourning family to eat. After several refusals, justified by their very great sorrow, in the end the relatives of the dead woman consented to eat the 'bread of mourning' and drink 'the cup of consolation' (Jer. 16: 7; Hos. 9: 4).

The cave of Machpelah, Abraham's family tomb

This cave of Machpelah, in which the mortal remains of Sarah were laid, was to figure in the future as the family vault of Abraham's family. For here were to be laid, in

The cenotaphs of biblical patriarchs, in the mosque at Hebron

the course of the following centuries, Abraham, then his son Isaac together with his wife Rebekah and, lastly, Jacob (called Israel), Isaac's son, beside Leah, his first wife. Rachel, his second wife, was not laid in this tomb; she was buried by the wayside as the caravan, coming from the Upper Euphrates, made its way to Hebron.

At Mamre, Abraham's camp was established, it will be remembered, on the present site of the Haram Ramet el-Khalil (or hill sanctuary of the Friend of God). Abraham's well and the sacred enclosure can be seen there, partially surrounded by ancient walls made of enormous stones. It was here that the patriarch's tents stood and that Sarah breathed her last.

The cave of Machpelah was about two and a half miles to the south of the Hebrew camp under the oaks of Mamre, near the present village of Jebel er-Remeideh which is supposed to be the former village of Hebron. But the place has by no means retained its primitive appearance; a fortified mosque occupies the site of Ephron the Hurrite's field, and the tomb of the patriarchs constitutes the crypt of the mosque. In fact the present sanctuary is made up of three distinct parts: the external wall, the mosque and the tomb in the crypt.

The subsequent history of the cave of Machpelah

It has had a chequered history. The fact that we do not possess all the necessary information about the internal arrangement of this crypt must be ascribed to human turbulence. The following short résumé of events makes this clear.

Already in A.D. 333–4 the manuscript known as the Bordeaux Pilgrim mentions the presence of a mausoleum (*memoria*), above the cave of Machpelah, square in shape and beautifully constructed of stone. St Jerome, a tireless visitor of the holy places, confirms the statement.

Two centuries later a considerable change had occurred: Antoninus of Piacenza (570) describes his admiration for a basilica which at that period stood above the cave.

Seventy years later the tomb of the three patriarchs passed into the hands of the Mohammedans whose dominion extended to the whole of Palestine. But they do not seem, at least for a time, to have prevented Christians from going to pray there, though, of course, the former church was transformed into a mosque.

A further change occurred in 1099 when the Franks took possession of the country. The mosque was returned to use as a Christian sanctuary dedicated to St Abraham. This church was served at first by a college of canons governed by a prior. A little later it became a cathedral under a bishop. Pilgrims crowded to the spot and many of them have left descriptions of the building. In 1187 there was a further change of fortune and Saladin, the great Mohammedan leader, the conqueror of the Franks, hastened to reoccupy the tomb of Abraham, venerated by the followers of Allah both as a prophet and the father of Ishmael, the ancestor of the Arabs. Access to the cave was not, however, forbidden to Christians, at least according to the account drawn up by the Dominican Buchard (1283) who seems to have been given permission to spend a whole night in prayer by the tomb of the patriarchs. But in 1583 the Franciscan Quaresimus notes with understandable grief the formal prohibition of all visits to the crypt. In fact from the sixteenth century down to the middle of the nineteenth no Christian was able to enter the cave of Machpelah.

In 1843, however, Dr Frankel succeeded in bribing the keepers of the underground sanctuary; he went down into the crypt and was able to observe the sarcophagi, each of which, bearing the name of a patriarch cut in Hebrew and Arabic letters, was covered in damask.

The last European investigation, carried out with uncommon daring, took place in 1859. Its hero was the Piedmontese architect Pierotti, at that time an official of the municipality of Jerusalem. Disguised as an Arab and with the complicity of the keeper of the tomb, purchased for a considerable sum, he managed to effect an attempted descent. According to his account the principal staircase goes down from the vestibule of the mosque. It comes out above, and nearly in the centre, of the ancient cave. It is hewn out of the rock and is only a little over two feet wide. It terminates in a large iron grill heavily padlocked. The keeper, despite the large bribe paid by Pierotti, only allowed him to go down five steps. From this point, in the light of the lamps [7] which light up the tomb continuously, he could make out some sarcophagi of white stone. All this, it must be admitted, provides but scanty information.

Since then there have been several attempts to go down into the tomb which, despite preparation by official and diplomatic channels, have been fruitless.

Isaac's marriage

Sarah had been laid in the tomb. Abraham, whom 'Yahweh had blessed in every way', was now an old man well on in years, and Isaac, the patriarch's son, would soon, in the nature of things, be called upon to assume the shepherd's crook as head of the clan. But Isaac, the only son on whom was founded every hope for the continuance of the line, had not yet chosen a wife.

Abraham made up his mind: Isaac must have a wife. And he must not marry one of the daughters of the Canaanites, with their idolatrous religion and its bloodthirsty and licentious rites. He should have a pure bred

[7] These lamps are let down by a cord from the floor of the mosque built above the cave, through six openings no more than a foot wide. The oil for the lamps is paid for by gifts coming from all over the Islamic world.

Family Affairs

Aramean, one of the nomads belonging to the tribes of shepherds living on the Mesopotamian steppes, or, and this would be nearer to hand, on the vast green plains of the Upper Euphrates round Haran, the great pastoral centre. In short, one of the kinsfolk of the Hebrews. Of course, these tribes, too, were worshippers of false gods, but mutual understanding was easier with them. So the patriarch called to him his eldest and most trusted servant, his steward, traditionally supposed to be Eliezer, and said to him: *'Place your hand under my thigh*[8], *I would have you swear by Yahweh, God of heaven and God of earth, that you will not choose a wife for my son from the daughters of the Canaanites among whom I live. Instead go to my own land and my own kinfolk to choose a wife for my son Isaac.'*

Now implicit in this order was a danger. Both Abraham and Eliezer were aware of it. According to Babylonian law, in fact, the girl who was chosen was obliged to accept the husband given to her by her father. On the other hand, she was free to refuse to join her husband's clan; in that case it was for the husband to come and join his father-in-law's clan.

Abraham's delegate, who had no wish to find himself in difficulties, asked for fuller instructions: *'What if the woman does not want to come with me to this country? Must I take your son back to the country from which you came?'* Abraham's answer was clear: in no case must Isaac return to the land of his fathers. *'Yahweh, God of heaven and God of earth, took me from my father's home, and from the land of my kinsfolk, and he swore to me that he would give this country* [Canaan] *to my descendants. He will now send his angel ahead of you, so that you may choose a wife for my son there.'* In conclusion, Abraham gave a final warning: *'Do not take my*

[8] Touching the genital organs was meant to make the oath inviolable.

son back there.' The reason for this is quite clear: for the clan of Yahweh's adherents to return among the tribes which though kinsfolk of Abraham's were still plunged in their idolatrous beliefs, would amount, quite simply, to the failure of God's plan and the abrupt halting of the spiritual progress of the Chosen People.

Thereupon, with a troop of ten camels taken from those belonging to his master, Eliezer started on his journey taking 'something of the best of all his master owned' (in other words, some ingots of gold and silver, and a few jewels – all this to provide the dowry, or, in plain words, the purchase price of the girl). Eliezer set out straight for Aram-Naharaiim 'and the town of Nahor' the Bible tells us.

At the Oak of Mamre they were well aware that the clan of Nahor, Abraham's brother, was grazing his flocks in the pleasant valleys of the Upper Euphrates and that the family was very prosperous. It is even very probable that the existence of Rebekah, Nahor's daughter or grand-daughter [9], was not unknown in Abraham's family, and this despite the distance separating these two groups of shepherds.

Eliezer arrived outside Haran and halted his party at the gates of the city. *In the evening, at the time when women go down to draw water, he made the camels kneel . . . near the well. Abraham's slave entrusted the matter to Yahweh: 'God of my master Abraham,' he prayed, 'be with me today, and show your kindness to my master Abraham.'* In all simplicity the patriarch's servant asked a sign of the Lord. *'Here I stand by the*

---

[9] There are here two apparently contradictory traditions. According to certain passages of Chapter 24 Rebekah is the daughter of Bethuel the son of Milcah (verses 15, 24 and 47). Elsewhere (24: 48; 29: 5) she is described as the daughter of Nahor. The lack of precision of the Hebrew vocabulary in genealogical matters hardly needs emphasizing. It may have been noticed in passages quoted previously in this book that Abraham calls his nephew Lot his brother.

Rebekah may have looked like this

spring,' he went on, *'as the young women from the town come out to draw water. To one of the girls I will say: Please tilt your pitcher and let me drink. If she answers, "Drink, and I will water your camels too," may she be the one you have chosen for your servant Isaac; by this I shall know you have shown your kindness to my master'* (Gen. 24: 12–14).

The biblical account states that he had not finished speaking when Rebekah came out to draw water from the well; she was very beautiful and a virgin. Eliezer went straight up to her and asked her to give him water. *She replied, 'Drink, my Lord,' and quickly lowered her pitcher on her arm and gave him a drink.* Then she offered to draw water for his camels also. Quickly she emptied her pitcher into the trough, ran again to the well and drew water for all the camels. Eliezer considered her in silence, wondering whether Yahweh had or had not brought him to the end of his quest.

The animals had finished drinking. Eliezer now took a gold ring weighing half a shekel and put it through Rebekah's nostrils. This was the *nezem* (for the nose), an open ring, attached to the cartilage separating the nostrils, and worn by women from the right nostril. Then on her wrist he placed two golden bracelets, each weighing ten shekels. Then Eliezer questioned her: *'Whose daughter are you? Please tell me. Is there room at your father's house for us to spend the night?'* Her answer was unexpected: *'I am the daughter of Bethuel, the son whom Milcah bore to Nahor.'* Thus Eliezer found himself among the descendants of Terah and could not have chosen better. Rebekah went on: *'We have plenty of straw and fodder, and room to lodge.'* And the Bible adds: *Then the man bowed down and worshipped Yahweh saying, 'Blessed be Yahweh, God of my master Abraham, for he has not stopped showing kindness and goodness to my master. Yahweh has guided my steps to the house of my master's brother.'*

Rebekah ran at once to her mother and her brother and told of the stranger who was soon to arrive. [10] Laban hastened out to Eliezer, who remained standing by the well with his camels. *'Why stay out here,'* he inquired, *'when I have cleared the house and made room for the camels?'* And so Eliezer was conducted to the house. [11] Although Laban possessed a considerable staff of slaves, he made a point of himself unloading the camels and providing them with straw and fodder. The animals had to be attended to first. After this he brought water for the travellers to wash their feet, and invited Eliezer to a meal. But Abraham's servant refused politely, at least for the moment, to eat anything before the whole of his story was told. In truly eastern fashion he recounted all Abraham's adventures as a wandering shepherd; he stated in detail the immense resources of his master, *flocks and herds, silver and gold, men slaves and women slaves, camels and donkeys'.* He related the belated birth of Isaac, described the sacred mission with which he had been charged, and expressed his wonder that directly on arrival he encountered at the well at the city gates the *daughter of my master's brother.* He concluded: *'Now tell me whether you are prepared to show kindness and*

[10] Nahor, Abraham's brother, and father (or grandfather) of Rebekah, does not appear in any of the following scenes. We shall probably be right in regarding him as already dead at the time when Eliezer arrived with his ten camels at Haran. Then there is Bethuel whom certain verses mention as Rebekah's father. In fact, Bethuel is mentioned a little further on. But biblical scholars, including the Dominicans of the Ecole Biblique, think that Bethuel was added at a later date. On the one hand he crops up very incidentally; on the other, it is Laban, Rebekah's brother, who in all the following negotiations appears as the head of the family. He acts as 'patriarch' in treating of his sister's marriage and seems to possess full powers to carry out these delicate negotiations, a power which was jealously reserved, according to the law of these shepherds, to the head of the clan.

[11] This is an example of the family of a chieftain, the owner of large flocks and employing shepherds and slaves, dwelling within a city (Haran). This was one of the stages towards settling permanently in one place; the same thing applies to Lot at Sodom. On the other hand, Abraham and the patriarchs, his descendants, always remained faithful to camp life in a tent.

goodness to my master; if not, say so, and I shall know what to do.

The answer came at once; it was favourable to Eliezer's request. Thereupon he unpacked and *brought out silver and gold ornaments and clothes which he gave to Rebekah*; these were gifts for her betrothal to Isaac. In addition, *he gave rich presents to her brother and to her mother*; this was the traditional and obligatory payment made to the parents of the future wife. The Babylonian code fixed this payment (the 'price', in fact, of the girl) at fifty shekels of gold. Deuteronomy mentions the same sum. By the acceptance of this sum by the parents, the woman, whose consent had been asked by no one, from that instant belonged to the future husband, Isaac.

The next day when the household was up Eliezer asked permission to leave with Rebekah and return to the far distant camp at Hebron. Rebekah was called and questioned by her brother Laban: *'Do you want to leave with this man?' 'I do,' she replied. Accordingly they let their sister Rebekah go, with her nurse, and Abraham's servant and his men.*

At the time of the patriarchs it appears that marriage was not marked by any special ceremony. There was merely the blessing given by the head of the clan when the bride to be left her own people to found a new family. After this the small party under Eliezer's leadership set out on the way back.

The Hebrew camp was temporarily established in the Negeb at the well of Lahai Roi (Gen. 24: 62–6). Now one evening as night fell Isaac was walking to the north of the camp, anxious, probably, about Eliezer's mission and the arrival of the party. Suddenly on the horizon he saw the line of camels. Rebekah, too, must have been watching for the tents to come into sight. From afar off she noticed the solitary walker. At once she jumped from the camel and in curiosity, and probably with some anxiety also, inquired of Eliezer: *'Who is that man walking through the fields to meet us?'* He replied, *'That is my master.'* Hurriedly, Rebekah covered her face with the traditional veil which, as was customary, she was to wear until her wedding night. *Isaac led Rebekah into his tent and made her his wife; and he loved her*.

Abraham's further descendants

After Sarah's death, Abraham, the patriarch who had been described as an old man unable to have any more children, took another wife, not a legitimate wife, but a concubine. Her name was Keturah. She bore Abraham six sons whose names the Bible records, to explain the origins of a group of Arab tribes.

Keturah's children were endowed by Abraham; he gave them flocks, and as soon as possible, took care to see that they left the camp. *During his lifetime,* Genesis tells us, *he sent them away from his son Isaac eastward, to the east country*. According to tradition the sons of Keturah became the ancestors of the tribes of southern Arabia. Ishmael, the son of Hagar the concubine, was sent away from the camp, as we know; down in the wilderness of Haran he was to appear as the ancestor of the Ishmaelite Arabs.

In fact the promise made by God to Abraham applied only to Isaac, the patriarch's sole heir; in his veins ran pure Hebrew blood, free from any taint of misalliance. And indeed it was necessary for the accomplishment of this stage of the mission that there should be only one leader. After Abraham came Isaac; after Isaac, Jacob; to form the succession of biblical patriarchs.

Abraham joins Sarah in the cave of Machpelah

Abraham, the Bible informs us, *breathed his last, dying at a ripe old age, an old man who had lived his full span of years*. We are told that for the patriarch's burial, Ishmael, probably warned in good time, hastened to his half-brother Isaac to pay funeral honours to his father. The heavy boulder obstructing the entrance to the cave of Machpelah was rolled aside and, on a stone shelf next to that on which Sarah's body lay, the mortal remains of Abraham, the one loved by God, were laid to rest in the curled position favoured by tradition.

EPILOGUE

Abraham's religious life, which governs the future spiritual evolution of the Chosen People, was marked by three events of great significance:

Firstly, the choosing of Abraham by the Lord.

Next, the Covenant made between God and Abraham (and his descendants).

Lastly, Abraham's faithfulness. His was integral, unshakable faith, a whole-hearted acceptance of the mission entrusted to him by God. Abraham's earthly life was over. The history of the Chosen People now began.

SELECT BIBLIOGRAPHY

The Jerusalem Bible: Darton, Longman & Todd (London), Doubleday and Company Inc. (New York)

General Books

A Catholic Commentary on Holy Scripture; Nelson (London)

Peake's Commentary on the Bible (Revised Edition); Nelson (London)

L. H. Grollenburg, O.P.: *Atlas of the Bible;* Nelson (London)

R. de Vaux, O.P.: *Ancient Israel;* Darton, Longman & Todd (London), McGraw-Hill Book Company (New York)

J. L. McKenzie, S.J.: *Dictionary of the Bible;* Chapman (London), The Bruce Publishing Co. (Milwaukee)

J. Bright: *A History of Israel;* S.C.M. Press (London), Westminster Press (Philadelphia)

T. Maertens: *Bible Themes;* Darton, Longman & Todd (London), Fides Publishers Inc. (Indiana)

C. Charlier: *The Christian Approach to the Bible;* Sands Publishers (Glasgow)

Books about Genesis

J. Blenkinsopp: *From Adam to Abraham;* Darton, Longman & Todd (London), Paulist Press (New York)

G. von Rad: *Genesis;* S.C.M. Press (London), Westminster Press (Philadelphia)

J. Rhymer: *The Beginnings of a People;* Sheed & Ward (London), Pflaum Press (Dayton, Ohio)

A. Richardson: *Genesis;* S.C.M. Press (London), the Macmillan Company (New York)

B. Vawter: *A Path through Genesis;* Sheed & Ward (London)

INDEX OF NAMES

187

Index of Names

INDEX OF PLACES

Index of Places

Index of Places

Nihil obstat: John M. T. Barton, S.T.D., L.S.S., Censor
Imprimatur: Patrick Casey V.G.
Westminster, 22 July 1968

Abraham,
Loved by God

by HENRI GAUBERT

Translated by Lancelot Sheppard

A Giniger Book
published in association with
HASTINGS HOUSE, PUBLISHERS
NEW YORK